DEDICATION

*To the future-
Suzanne, Marty, Michael, "B.J."
Aleta & Nova*

*To the past-
In loving memory of our
super-talent "Chuck"*

*And to the thousands of talented
percussionists who passed through
the portals of Franks Drum Shop*

ISBN 978-1-888408-55-3

© 1993 Maurie Lishon and Rebeats Publications

This is a Rebeats publication, edited and produced by Rob Cook,
who is soley responsible for its content and distribution.

REBEATS
P.O. Box 6, Alma, Michigan 48801 www.rebeats.com

AN EASY PLACE TO MISS IF YOU WEREN'T WATCHING FOR IT!

The front entrance to the building that housed Franks Drum Shop, as it looked in about 1960. This photo was taken just after Maurie won a fight to have a directory mounted on the ground floor.

Preface

Unlike countless numbers of customers who traveled great distances (sometimes thousands of miles) to get to Franks Drum Shop, I found it by accident. It was 1966, and I was sixteen. I'd been playing drums since 4th grade and was dying to get my first professional outfit. My dad was making me wait until I had the money saved up. Dad was now in Chicago on an annual buying trip for his office-supply store, and I got to tag along. As we walked down Wabash Avenue on the way to the hotel, my dad noticed the little listing on the directory at 226 South-"Franks Drum Shop 4th Flr". Dad wanted to check it out, but had to talk me into it. It seemed like a waste of time to me- I figured any store worth it's salt would have nice window displays on the ground floor, not just a barely noticeable line listing on a directory. My dad persisted, and I reluctantly followed him into the elevator at the end of the long and rather dingy hallway. What I saw when the elevator door opened on the fourth floor changed forever the way I thought about drums and drummers.

My dad is an outgoing "people person", and within minutes was introducing me to the shop's owner, Maurie Lishon. I was more than a little bewildered when this guy greeted me as if I were a relative or a famous pro.... We got a complete tour as Maurie showed us through his office with all it's pictures, the print music files, the back room crammed with unique effects devices, etc. It wasn't too hard to get my dad to change the game plan on my drum kit; he agreed that this was the time and place to buy my kit, and I could pay him back on an installment plan. From that day forward I would always refer to that kit not just as "a Ludwig Hollywood", but as "a Ludwig Hollywood I bought at Franks Drum Shop in Chicago-from Maurie Lishon". I bought lots more stuff from Franks, not only for myself but for friends and students. It always made me feel special to be able to call Franks and ask for Maurie. He'd always take my calls, and always wanted to know how things were going up in Michigan.

I'm not saying Maurie never jumped to the wrong conclusion, never offended anyone, never hurt anyone's feelings. I've seen him light into people-sometimes even family members. It was never cruel or mean-spirited, it's just that he had no patience whatsoever for incompetence, ignorance, or laziness, and he was quick to let you know what he was thinking. Like Buddy Rich, Maurie "suffered no fool gladly".

That's why, in my opinion, he inspired so many percussionists. You knew if you earned his approval you were probably on the right track.

Folks have been telling Maurie for 20 years that he should write a book. I'm proud that when he finally decided to do it that he called me to see if it was a project I wanted to get involved in. I just hope that this book does him proud.

Rob Cook

Table of Contents

CHAPTER ONE   THE DIXIE MUSIC HOUSE — 1
The beginnings of the business that would one day evolve into Frank's Drum Shop.

CHAPTER TWO   MAURIE LISHON — 11
Maurie's childhood and early playing career.

CHAPTER THREE   JANICE ROGERS-LISHON — 45
Jan's childhood and dancing career.

CHAPTER FOUR   CHUCK LISHON   1941-1978 — 49
Maurie and Jan's eldest son; an incredible talent who died at a tragically young age.

CHAPTER FIVE   MAURIE BUYS FRANK'S — 55
Frank Gault passes the baton to Maurie, who expands, then moves down to the 4th floor.

CHAPTER SIX   EQUIPMENT — 75
Some notes on the equipment Maurie used and sold.

CHAPTER SEVEN   THE MYSTIQUE OF FRANKS — 81
The clinics and customer service that made Franks a legend in the industry.

CHAPTER EIGHT   ROY C KNAPP — 99
The life story of 'Uncle Roy' - America's dean of percussion and an important part of Franks Drum Shop.

CHAPTER NINE   KRUPA, RICH, & BELLSON — 109
Three of America's most famous drummers; their associations with Franks.

CHAPTER TEN   THE SECOND TIME AROUND — 125
Maurie sells the shop to son Marty and moves to Florida where he picks up the sticks again.

APPENDIX — 133
The students of Roy C Knapp; a complete listing

MESSAGES FROM FRIENDS — 149
Photos and anecdotes from many of the world's leading percussionists.

Chapter One
THE DIXIE MUSIC HOUSE

While Boston was probably the center of the 'Drumming Universe' in the first part of the 20th century what with George Stone, Oliver Ditson, Harry Bower and many others active there, there's not much doubt that the Chicago area (include Elkhart in there!) was the center of the rest of the musical universe.

Almost every major city had a huge 'music company'. These firms (usually several stories high) were basically retail stores. Equally important, however, were the mail-order and manufacturing departments. Many of these emporiums made their own drums, pianos, banjos, and other instruments. (Even more common was the practice of purchasing 'OEM' products- instruments supplied by the manufacturer with a dealer's custom nameplate so that it appeared to have been manufactured by this dealer.)

Our story begins with such an operation. Well- not quite. Actually we have to go back just a few years earlier, to the city of New Orleans.

Three of the cornet (note; this does not mean trumpet!) players with 'Brook's Chicago Marine Band' put their heads together and conceived of a plan to start an agency for booking talent and services.

By the time they actually started doing business in Chicago as the 'Dixie Music House', they'd decided to sell merchandise. Establishing a tradition that would remain for seven decades, the focus was set on the professional musician; the trio wanted to service bands and bandmen exclusively.

The best known of the three was Bert Brown. Brown was a soloist with the popular Arthur Pryor's band for twelve years, and played for a time with the Sousa band. His solos on the cornet with the big pipe organ and orchestra at the McVickers theater made him famous in Chicago. Many times he stopped the regular show to respond to encores demanded by the audience.

The second partner was Hubert Darrow. It was Hubert's brother who would be responsible for putting the Darrow name in the history books-Clarence Darrow became one of the most famous names in American legal history.

The third partner was George C Gault of Chicago.

George C Gault

co-founder,
Dixie Music House

Dixie Music House got rolling in about 1900 at 125 N Fifth Avenue. (For those of you familiar with Chicago, today this is Wells). George's younger brother Frank was 10 years old. Frank started to work at Dixie in 1903 at the age of 13.

In those first years the Dixie didn't carry much inventory, as it was so easy for them to pick up the short items locally.

Printed music was an important part of the Dixie's business. They not only distributed, but published (and even, in some cases, composed) the music. The xylophone/piano piece 'Margellen' listed in the ad here was by Frank Gault.

Another rapidly growing enterprise at the same address was a shop on the seventh floor. Here William and Theobald Ludwig had opened a shop primarily to introduce the bass drum foot pedal they had invented. The Ludwig brothers also were exclusive Chicago agents for the Leedy Drum Company of Indianapolis.

Dixie Music House continued to grow, becoming the type of operation mentioned earlier; a large mail-order catalog was put together and the constantly increasing inventory forced two more moves; first to 105 W Madison, and finally to 326 S Wabash. Percussion had become a significant portion of the store's total business, and Dixie serviced most of the Chicago and area drummers. Part of the reason for this was the excellent repair department. Excellent facilities and repairmen mixed with a lot of percussion know-how were making them famous, which brought increasingly odd and exotic requests.

Some of the special projects that Frank remembered the shop producing:

- A chime hammer with a four-foot handle for Roy Knapp. (This was so Roy could handle the Chime parts without getting out of his seat. Previous to this he had used a chime mallet tied to a broom handle.)

-A two-octave set of tuned skillets for Harry Budinger. These ranged from 4" to 16" in diameter, so by the time they were racked up they took up so much space that Budinger had to wear roller skates to play them.

-A special seat for Otto Kristufek to use when playing his Dresden pedal tympani.

-Numerous sets of tuned items; cowbells, wood blocks, etc. (They had to pass on a call for two octaves of triangle.)

The manager of the drum department was Edward B Straight, who was very much a personality even then. (The 'Ed Straight System of Drumming' would become one of the biggest selling drum instructional books in the country.) Within 5 years more space was needed, so Dixie Music House moved to 134 W Van Buren St where space was shared with Local 10 of the Chicago Federation of Musicians. Frank Gault joined the union in 1906 at 16 as a trombone player. Though he was an excellent trombonist, he wound up working in the drum department at Dixie.

Frank Gault

As seen on the next few pages (from a 1921 catalog), the Dixie Music House carried a large selection of special effects for the theater drummer.

KEEP THIS CATALOG FOR REFERENCE
New Pages Will Be Supplied As Fast As We Publish Them

B-1-1393

THE DRUMMER'S VADE MECUM

A COMPLETE AND UP-TO-DATE CATALOG OF DRUMS, TRAPS AND DRUMMERS' SUPPLIES

DIXIE MUSIC HOUSE DRUM DEPARTMENT CATALOG COVER, 1921
(This was a loose-leaf catalog; page changes could be made at a moment's notice.)

The Dixie Music House

"THE BANDMAN'S HOUSE"
105 West Madison Street
320 S. WABASH AVE.
CHICAGO

DIXIE MUSIC HOUSE DRUM DEPARTMENT CATALOG INDEX 1921
Note the dozens of sound-effects devices designed for
the theater drummer providing sound for silent films.

INDEX

A READY REFERENCE GUIDE TO THE
DRUMMERS' VADE MECUM

A Complete and Up-To-Date Catalog of
DRUMMERS' SUPPLIES

INDEX

Article	Page
Air Brake	56
Airplane Imitation	56
Alarm Clock	59
All Metal Drum Repair Parts	47
All Metal Snare Drums	4-5
Aluminum Spurs	43
Ambulance Gong	58-61
Analysis of 6-8 Time	35
Anchor (Heaving)	57
Anvils	58
Automatic Cymbal Muffler	17
Automobile Horn	57
Baby Cry	54, 61
Bags, Drum	20
Bantam Rooster	20
Bass Drum Cases	45
Bass Drum Music Racks	9, 10, 11, 12
Bass Drums	9, 10, 11, 12
Bass Drum Sticks	36
Batons, Drum Major's	50
Bear Growl	59
Beaters, Cymbal	45
Beaters, Bass Drum	36
Beaters, Drum and Cymbal	17, 18
Bee Hum	62
Bell Mallets	37
Bell Methods	35
Bell Plates	58
Bell Solos	35
Bells, Orchestra	21, 22, 23, 24, 25
Bells, Song	25
Bell Stands	44
Belts	43
Bicycle Bell	59
Bicycle Whistle	55
Bird Whistles	60
Block Holders	46, 52
Bob White	56
Braces, Drum	43
Breaking Glass Effect	57
Bugle Cord	49
Bugle Methods	35
Bugles	49
Bugle Sling	49
Burglar Alarm	59
Buzzer	62
Calf Bawl	54
Carnival Rooster	56
Cases, Bass Drum	20
Cases, Bell	21, 25
Cases, Cathedral Chimes	33
Cases, Music Stand	48
Cases, Snare Drum	19, 20
Cases, Tubaphone	33
Cases, Xylophone	26, 28, 29
Castanets	60
Cathedral Chimes	33, 61
Cathedral Chimes Method	35
Cat Meow	62
Cavalry Horse	58, 59, 61
Center Supports, Drum Rod	37
Champagne Pop	54
Chime Mallets	37
Chime Methods	35

Article	Page
Chimes	33, 61
Chinese Cymbals	39, 63
Chinese Gongs	63
Chinese Horns	63
Chinese Musettes	63
Chinese Skin Drums	63
Chinese Tom Toms	63
Chinese Wood Block Holder	46
Chinese Wood Blocks	63
Chromatic Pitch Pipe (for tympani)	47
Church Bell	58
Clock Tick	60
Clock (Winding)	56
Clog Mallets	61
Combination Jazz Sets	12, 52
Comedy Slide Whistles	55, 56
Concert Bass Drums	11
Conditions of Sale	3d page of cover
Cord, Bugle	49
Cord, Drum	43
Cord Hooks	43
Cornet Jazzers	53
Counter Hoops	47
Cover for Pedal Ball	18
Cow Bawl	54, 61
Cow Bell Holders	46, 51, 52
Cow Bells	51
Crane (Hoisting)	57
Crash Cymbal Holders	40, 41
Crash Cymbals	39, 63
Credit	3d page of cover
Cricket	62
Crow Caw	61
Crushing Effect	56
Cuckoo	56
Cyclone Whistle	55
Cymbal Beaters	45
Cymbal Brackets	40
Cymbal Clamps	40
Cymbal Holders	40, 41
Cymbal Muffler	17
Cymbals	39, 63
Derrick Imitation	57
Devilene (Sirene Whistle)	55
Disappearing Spurs	43
Dog Bark	57, 59
Door Bell	59
Double End Bass Drum Sticks	36
Drum and Cymbal Beaters (Pedals)	17, 18
Drum Bags	20
Drum Bell	59
Drum Belts and Slings	43
Drum Cases	19, 20
Drum Chart	55
Drum Cord	43
Drum Ears (Braces)	47
Drum Head Mending Tissue	20
Drum Head Protector (Fibre)	31
Drum Heads	44
Drum Head Tucker	44
Drum Heater	45
Drum Hooks	43
Drum Hoops	47
Drum Keys and Wrenches	43, 47

Article	Page
Drum Major's Batons	50
Drum Major's Whistle	55
Drummer's Special Xylophone	28
Drum Methods	45
Drum Music Racks	45
Drum Rods	37
Drums, Bass	9, 10, 11, 12
Drums, Concert Bass	11
Drums, Field	7, 8
Drum Shells	47
Drums, Kettle	13, 14, 15, 16
Drum Snares	42
Drum Spurs	43
Drums, Regimental	7, 8
Drums, Snare	1, 2, 3, 4, 5, 6, 7, 8
Drums, Street Model	7, 8
Drum Stands	38
Drum Sticks	36
Duck Quack	61
Dunghill Rooster	54
Ears, Drum	43
Electric Drum Heater	45
Electric Planing Mill	57
Elephant Trumpet	59
Elevator	57
Ferry Boat Whistle	55
Fibre Drum Cases	19, 20
Fibre Drum Head Cover	20
Field Drums	7, 8
Fife Methods	35
Fife Mouthpieces	50
Fifes	50
Fire Engine Gong	58, 61, 62
Fire Engine Whistle	55
Flesh Hoops	47
Fly Buzz	62
Fog Horn	55
Four Hammer Xylophone Solos	35
Four Tone Wood Blocks	52, 53
Freight Elevator	57
Frisco Song Whistle	56
Galloping Horses	58
Game Call	61
Gate (Closing)	56
Gear Effect	57
Glass Crash	57
Gong Holder	46
Gongs	58, 61, 63
Great Lakes Steamer Whistle	55
Hand Cymbal Holder	40
Heads	34, 39
Heater, Drum	45
Heaving the Anchor	57
Hen Cackles	54, 61
Hoisting Gear Effect	57
Holders (various)	40, 41, 46, 51, 52, 60
Hooks, Drum	43, 47
Hoops, Drum	47
Horse Hoofs	59
Horse Hoof Slab	59
Horse Neigh	61
Humanatone	62

5

1921 DIXIE MUSIC HOUSE DRUM DEPARTMENT CATALOG
Some of the sound-effects devices for 'picture show drummers'

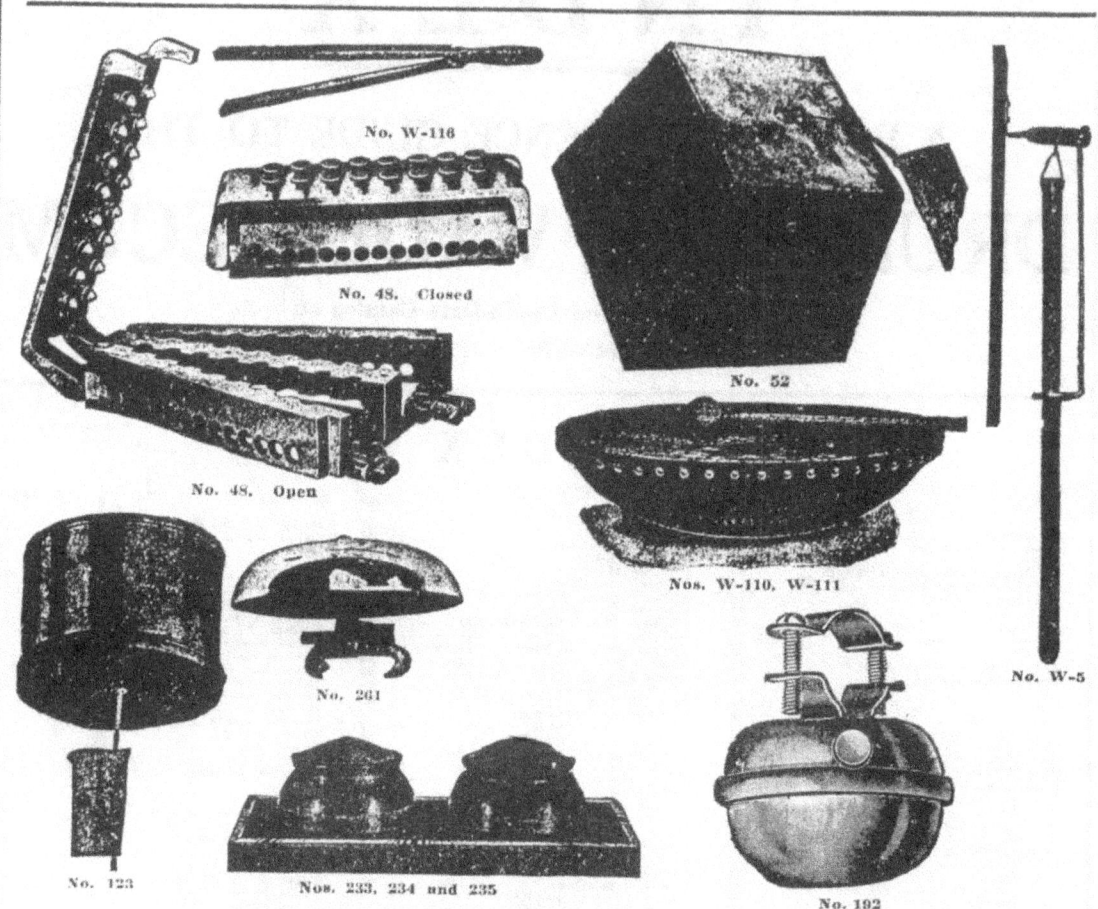

DRUMMERS' TRAPS

No. W-116. **Slap Stick or Whip Crack.** Works with one hand. Loud, durable and a perfect imitation. Made of hardwood, nicely finished .... $......

No. 48. **Shot Machine.** A practical shooting device that eliminates all pistol troubles. Absolutely safe and sure. Lifting the cover empties the machine, ready for reloading. Holds sixteen .32 calibre blanks; can be reloaded in 30 seconds. Nothing to get out of order. Made of Aluminum. Size, 6x2x2 inches...

No. 52. **Lion Roar, Etc.** Indispensable to Picture Show Drummers, for Lion Roar, Bear Growl, Elephant Trumpet and other Jungle effects. Size, 8x10 inches. Best Calf Head, gut cord and rosin pad..

No. W-5. **Locomotive Bell**...Perfect Imitation. Complete, with hammer..

No. W-110. **Indian Drum.** Band size..

No. W-111. **Indian Drum.** Orchestra size..

No. 123. **Dog Bark.** Perfect Imitation. Body made of tin, with four inch head..

No. 261. **Drum Bell** ("Snare Drum Cymbal"). Finest steel, nickel plated. Fastens to hoop..

No. 233. **Horse Hoofs.** Hand Turned Rock Maple, Half Round, with improved hand grip, doing away with strap handles. Per pair..

No. 234. **Horse Hoof Slab.** Specially constructed Slate Slab. 10½x5½ inches..

No. 235. No. 234 Slab and No. 233 Horse Hoofs, complete..

No. 192. **Telephone Bell, etc.** Electric movement, continuous ring, screw clamp. For Telephone Bell, Alarm Clock, Door Bell, Burglar Alarm, Bicycle Bell, etc. When muffled a perfect "buzzer" is secured. Takes up very little space (illustration is ¾ size)..

FOR PRICES SEE ENCLOSED QUOTATION SHEET.

THE DIXIE MUSIC HOUSE, - - Chicago

1921 DIXIE MUSIC HOUSE DRUM DEPARTMENT CATALOG

DIXIE "TANGO SPECIAL" AND PICTURE SHOW DRUM

Designed and built especially for the DANCE and MOVING PICTURE Business. The first one we constructed was an instantaneous success, since which they have sold as fast as we can make them.

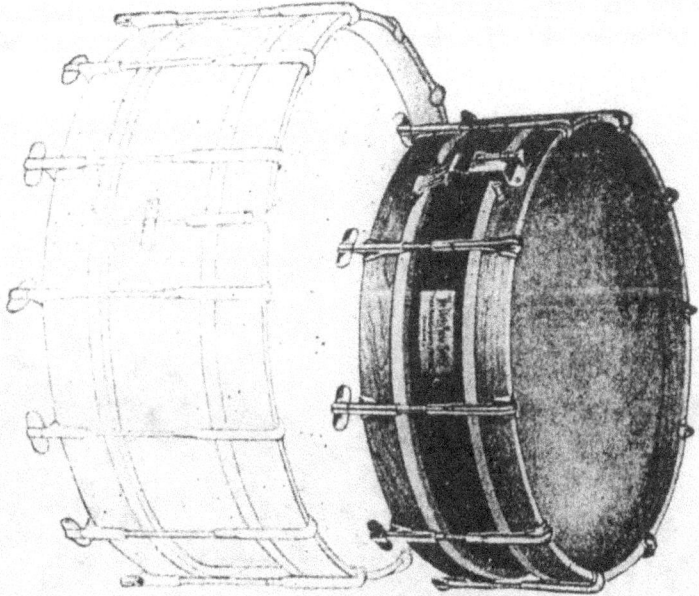

SNAPPY

DEPENDABLE

LOUD

CONVENIENT

INEXPENSIVE

UP-TO-DATE

A PERFECT DAMP-WEATHER DRUM

A WONDERFUL "JAZZER"

FINE FOR HOME USE
(With Piano or Talking Machine)

Illustration shows the TANGO SPECIAL in comparison with a 15 x 4 Drum of similar style

PRICE (Order No. 123) (Shipping weight 4 lbs., with case 9 lbs.)
State kind of Snares preferred.
Sticks not included.

FIBRE CASE, with 3 inch compartment at each end for traps (Order No. 277)...............

The DIXIE TANGO SPECIAL is the first and only Snare Drum ever produced to successfully meet the great demand created by the Dance, Moving Picture and general Small Orchestra Business for an entirely satisfactory Instrument.

The shell is of Walnut, 3 x 12 inches, fitted with finest XL Calf Heads, Thumb-screw Rods, Ludwig Patent Snare Strainer and Muffler. The Tone is so snappy as to be absolutely unequalled in that respect by any other Drum ever conceived, while at the same time the VOLUME is equal to that of a much larger and more expensive Drum.

In addition to the SUPERIORITY of this Drum, there are the Economical features to be considered—the small original cost, the saving in space, the reduction in weight (weighs only 3 lbs.), and the retrenchment in "upkeep" on account of fewer broken heads and the prevailing low cost of 15 inch heads.

TERMS: Send $2.00 deposit and we will ship C. O. D. with privilege of 5 days' trial, deducting the deposit from C. O. D. bill. For Prices see enclosed Quotation Sheet

THE DIXIE MUSIC HOUSE, - - Chicago

Tragedy struck on Thanksgiving eve of 1937 when the building on Wabash was totally destroyed by fire. The entire inventory of new instruments was lost as well as many customers' instruments in storage and in the repair shop. These losses included timpani belonging to Maurie Lishon, timpani belonging to Arthur Layfield (who was later to become percussionist with the New York Philharmonic), a five-octave marimba belonging to Milt Chalifaux, and many others.

After the fire at Dixie, Frank Gault was idle for only a couple of months. In January of 1938 he made the decision to open a special shop just for drummers.

Frank gave great credit to Arthur Steward for helping him get the shop opened. "Stu" had worked with, and for, Frank for 30 years already, and was to remain at his side until his retirement another 20 years later when Maurie Lishon bought the shop. During those 50 years, there would be only two periods during which Stu was not working with or for Frank. The first was 2 years during the first World War when he led his own (highly acclaimed) band. Later he spent 5 years as president of local 208. Frank also owed his start to financial help from E.J. Harrington. Harrington not only provided financial assistance, but physical help (muscle power!) and encouragement. This encouragement was much appreciated... Frank would later refer to Harrington as 'my angel'. (Maurie recalls that is was Ed Harrington who delivered the big rental instruments.)

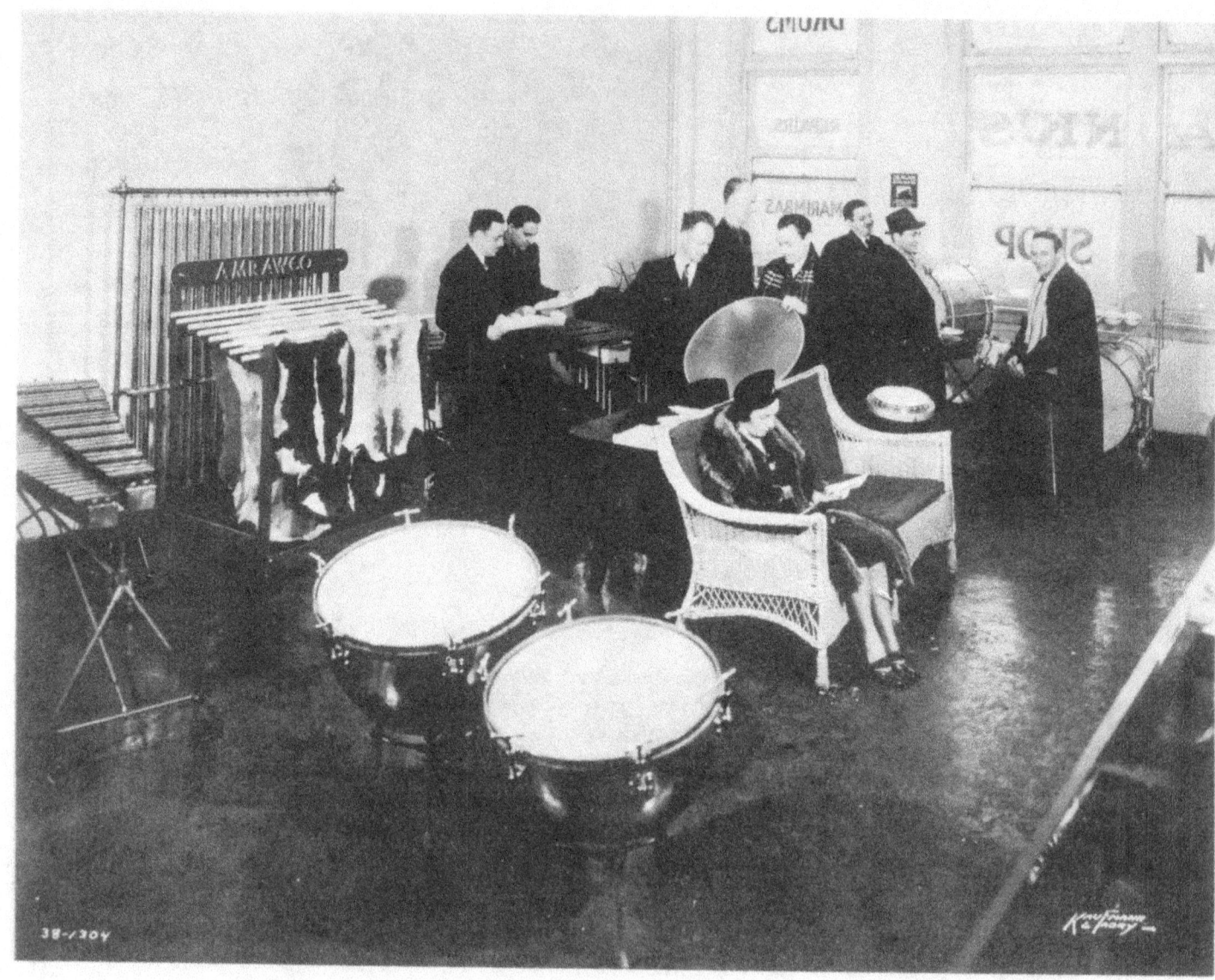

OPENING DAY, FRANK'S DRUM SHOP FEBRUARY 28, 1938
from left: Howard Emrie (American Rawhide), Ralph Smith (NBC), Frank Gault, John Noonan (player, teacher, Illinois Wesleyan University), Eddie Shebanek (Kay Kyser, Blackhawk), Bobby Christian, Maurie Lishon, Ormond Downes (Ted Weems). In foreground; Mrs Bobby (Jo) Christian

When Frank's Drum Shop opened, it wasn't as if someone came in and opened a brand new business from scratch.... Frank already had the personnel, the sources of supply, and even the clientele. It was as if the drum department from Dixie Music House had simply relocated. The business had been growing and developing for over 30 years, suffered a closure of several months, but reopened a block away in much larger quarters, on the fifth floor of 320 S Wabash.

The shop was immediately headquarters not only for local jobbing drummers, but any drummers who came to town. It was a wonderful place for drummers to 'catch the buzz' on the latest in the drum world and fraternize with players, teachers, and representatives from the manufacturers.

Phil Stanger began to 'hang out' and Frank's in about 1949, and says it was a real education just to sit back and listen to the theater drummers. "One of the first guys I met" says Phil, "was Alvin Stoller, who then was with Charlie Spivak's band."

This atmosphere was important to Frank, who helped foster the concept of the drummer's fraternity with annual get-togethers at the bar on the ground floor below his shop.

Front row, from left:
?, Joe Berryman, Frank Gault, ?, Warren Bills, Phil Grant, Sam Gayle
Back row, from left: Maurie Laurie, ?,?,Hal Kussius, Frank Pichl, Ed Metzenger, Bobby Christian, ?, Maurie Lishon, ?,?

DRUMMERS' PARTY
STAG

WEDNESDAY JUNE 4, 1947 - 9 P.M. UNTIL 3 A.M.

WONDERSPA BALCONY

226 S. WABASH AVE.

COMPLIMENTS

FRANK'S DRUM SHOP

Frank L. Gault   Joe Berryman

Maurie is in the center here, with the bow-tie. At his right is Joe Berryman. (Joe was Frank's partner for a time in the 40's when Frank needed operating capital.) Frank and Joe were jokingly referred to as the 'twin suits'. At Frank's right is his brother George, and in front of George (seated) is Ed Straight. At the other end of the bar, seated with the cigar, is Roy Knapp. Directly above Roy is George Way, and on Way's left is Wm F Ludwig Jr.

    While Frank's was a business that depended on making a profit like any other business, the customers never were subjected to a sales pitch or made to feel cooerced to purchase something they didn't really need. The key to Frank's success was that he simply helped educate the clientele as to what gear was available and appropriate for their needs. (Maurie continued the same policy.)

    Frank also helped with financing, carrying thousands of dollars 'on account' in the days before credit cards. He never sent out statements or set up formal payment plans; the customers paid what they could and did not take advantage of him. (Maurie continued this policy also, but 'policed' the charges more carefully.

    When the time came (22 years later) for Frank to retire, he spread the word that it would help him greatly if the accounts could be cleared up. Within 90 days over 75% of the $12,000.00 he was 'carrying' was paid off!

Chapter Two
Maurie Lishon

We got a little ahead of our story by looking at pictures of Maurie Lishon at the Frank's Drum Shop Wonderspa party. Maurie's story starts much, much earlier..... Here is his story, told in his own words:

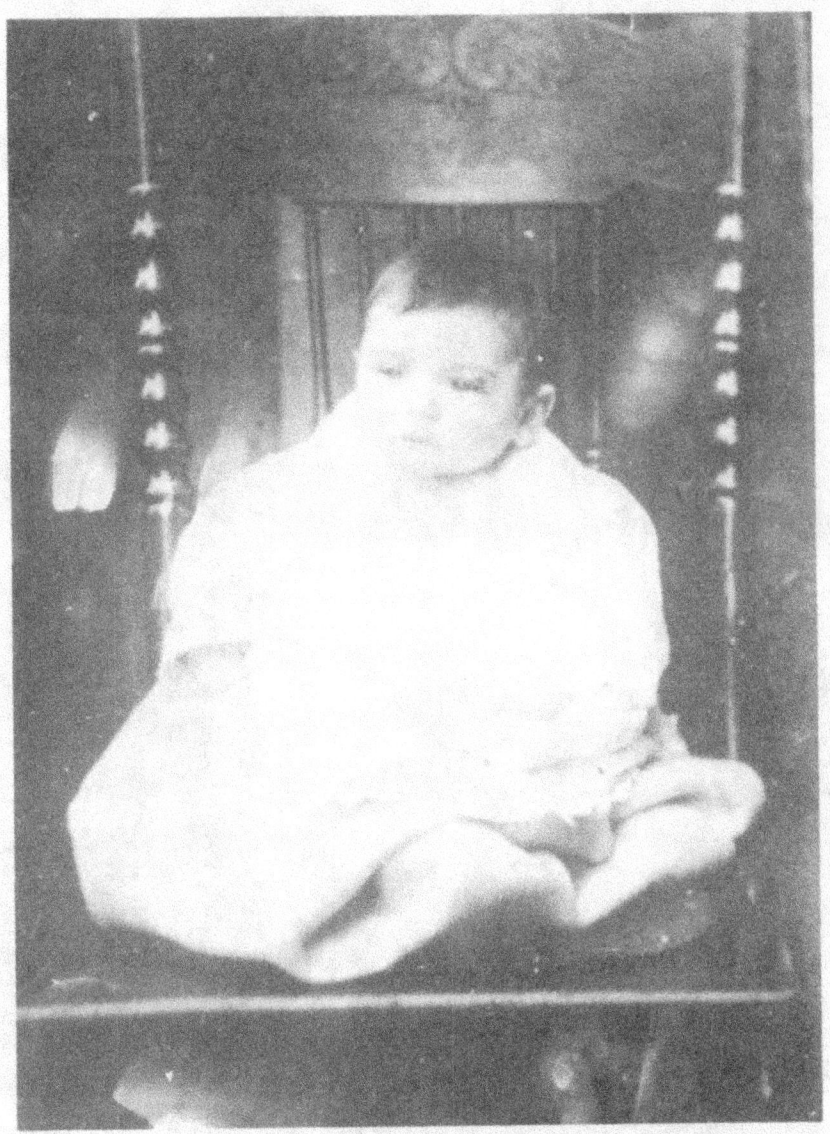

Maurice Lishon
born August 7th, 1914

I actually started playing when I was about 5 years old. I lived in a three-story building and we had a divider between our living room and dining room. There were some sheets of wood that were at the bottom of this thing-when you hit them with something it sounded like a snare drum to me. So I started out playing on that thing with knives and pencils; I got a great kick out of what I was doing and the sound I was making because I felt like I was really playing a drum.

When I went to grammar school, it was a place called Lafayette School in Chicago. I got into the orchestra in 3rd grade and I was in that orchestra for five years; my own graduation exercise was the 10th commencement exercise that I had played for. We had a wonderful music teacher by the name of Marie Sexton; she really gave me a lot of leeway and exposed me to semi-classical transriptions which called for tambourine parts and castanet parts, triangle parts- things like that. I remember I sat on a chair & my feet didn't even touch the floor. She was just wonderful, and by the time I graduated I'd been playing in that orchestra for 5 years, believe it or not.

The Lafayette Elementary School Orchestra in 1925, with Maurie Lishon on snare drum.

We used to get a big ribbon, and for every public affair that we played in the assembly hall we got a big gold star. Well- after 5 years I can't tell you how long that ribbon was, how many ribbons I had, or how many gold stars I had.

Occasionally, if a little job on the outside came up, we had a little group with two brothers- a fiddle player and a pianist- both excellent legitimate musicians; Treshansky was their name. So we organized the Sunshine Trio and occasionally we would get a pay job for two bucks. We played at the YMCA for free memberships and played little affairs there.

I had no drums or sticks or anything like that of my own, but Mrs Sexton would let me take the stuff out on the weekend when we had a little job to play & that 28" bass drum was bigger than I was. At the time it was just murder getting on the back of the streetcar- especially in the wintertime- and standing out there so nobody took my bass drum. (The streetcar cost 3 cents-this was in the early '20's.) In those days they used to have amateur nights at the theaters. (There were a lot of theaters in those days.) My brothers concocted the great idea to take me over- we rode over on the streetcar and were going to come back in a cab with my winnings.

I was supposed to dance to a song named "Angry", then I was going to get up and play the drums. Well, I got a little shy, and believe me, I blew the whole ball of wax. For my efforts all I got was about a twenty-cent box of candy. And now we have to get home, which was about a mile from the theater. We had blown our money getting TO the theater, so we had to walk back, and the boys made me carry the drums. That 28" bass drum was the heaviest bass drum I ever picked up in my life, to this day I remember it. So that was the beginning of my professional career in theater.

Let me clarify the dancing reference.... my older brother Jack (who has since passed away) won some kind of a contest and the prize was 12 tap dancing lessons. I used to watch him practice- he had about as much rhythm as, well- I can't even think, cause he had NO rhythm. He had no rhythm, but he SANG out of tune. Anyway, after watching him practice shuffle SHUFFLE shuffle SHUFFLE from foot to foot... by the time he got done with his twelve lessons I had learned a lot and I was a pretty good "hoofer". I could do time steps and I could do buck and wing and waltz clogs- I wound up with three or four routines that later, when I was working in smaller night clubs, if the soubrette got sick or one of the acts got sick, I'd go out, and I used to do imitations, I used to sing a little, and I would "hoof". In fact, in some of the clubs I worked, if we had a stripper that was sick that night or something, I would do a comedy strip to fill in that slot.

After I graduated from elementary school (and from that orchestra), I went to Crane Technical High School- an all boy's school, and I wanted to play in the band. As it happened, I was only about 4'8" and the smallest uniform, because it was ROTC, was for a kid 5' tall. Well I could play rings around the drummer in the band, but I had visions of my never getting to be 5" tall and I wasn't about to stay in the second band and be stuck with ROTC for four years. The only alternative I had (and I took it) was to flunk out of the band to get out of the ROTC, which turned out to be great for me. As it turned out, it allowed me to concentrate on what playing I did outside of school. That's when we started little dance bands & quartets & quintets-whatever you could get in instrumentation, that's what you had. We ended up with a little band that was called Mort Lond and his Londoners and we played for the dances in the community and it worked out pretty well.

My Father - *MY Display*   circa 1930

My father had fruit and vegetable stores and I had to work in the store and misc. hours that I could contribute because it was the only way I could pay my way back at home.

I played on the side wherever I could. Then, when it came time for me to graduate from high school and college came up, I wanted to be a journalist. But then it was a case of how do I do this.. What I did, was I worked for my father in the daytime and tried to pick up a job here and there wherever I could at night or reverse-if I worked in the store, went to school in the daytime, tried to play at night- it was kind of a mixed bag for a long time and half the time I didn't know where I was going.

Remember at this time I'd already been playing, or been exposed to drums, for about 13 years, and I sure wanted to play, but I still wanted to be a journalist. I tried Medill School of Journalism at Northwestern University night school one semester. I tried Crane College days for one semester, but it was trying to catch as catch can to work and support myself- it got a little rough. You must remember I'd been playing up til now 13 years and still hadn't taken any lessons- I could hardly read. I started getting these jobs with the Londoners these little night clubs where they would bring in acts. Well I had a very very good conception on tempos for one thing, and when we would talk over an act, I would write it out in long hand. If it was a dancing act, it was my meat because I knew the steps, if it was a singing act I just wrote it out in longhand; two and a half choruses, four bar tag, retard, hold, etc. I found many tricks that even helped me later on in my professional career because I had a very good reputation as a show drummer in later years in the Chicago area and it wound up to be my work playing theaters, night clubs, before I ever got into radio which was even long before television came on the scene in 1948.

Getting back to my journalism days, I had my own sports column for a couple of years in the Crane Tech Chronicle which was called Shorty's Sports Shorts and I also covered the Chicago public league football, baseball, basketball games for the prep editors of what was then the Chicago American and the Chicago Evening Post and I used to write these stories up for the men who were the prep editors in those days. All in all it gave me an element for writing and I developed a kind of a newspapery style which is what I wanted, but the journalism end didn't work out because after I had tried to get in to Northwestern and Crane College to further my journalism studies it just didn't work out 'cause I had to go to work.

During this period of time I also was manager of the championship city basketball teams at Crane High School and I was chosen as all-state cheerleader in 1930 and honorary manager of the all-star baseball team in the public school league at about the same time.

I'm now eighteen years old, through with school, and I've got to work- no question about that. Mort Lond and his Londoners were starting to make a little noise in the local areas (this is about 1933) and we got a job at Cedar Lake, Indiana, at a place called Surprise Park, for the summer. It was a wonderful summer- we learned a lot playing together, getting experience, and it worked out beautifully for us. Came September, and what are we gonna do? One of the people who had heard us at Surprise Park was a gentleman who owned a cabaret night club- a real swinging place just outside Hammond in Calumet City called "Dutch's".

The place had a tremendous reputation as a show club-they always had big shows and when Dutch and Max Snyder propositioned us to come to work we decided to take the job, so we moved into some fleabag hotel which was all that we could afford and took the job and now comes the question of the union.

Well... who's jurisdiction is it? Is it Chicago local, or Chicago Heights? And in those days Chicago Heights was headquarters for a lot of syndicate and what we used to refer to as gangster operations. Well, luckily, the Chicago local people, Jim Petrillo and company, won, so we joined the Chicago local. Otherwise, in later years, we would have had to transfer and go through all of that. But as it was, we joined the Chicago local and now we were members of local 10, Chicago Federation of Musicians, in good standing, all for 35 bucks a week. (This was 1934.)

At this point thing I should tell you that my father, rest his soul, (he was a wonderful man) had a thing about me being a musician. My older brother Henry was a dance band leader and show conductor and spent a lot of time on the road, and to my father with his old country ways that was a "gypsy" and he didn't want to see me be a "gypsy". As a result of which he never even bought me a pair of drumsticks- I don't know how I ever scraped up the money to buy a little here and a little there. Over a long period of time I built what was some semblance of an outfit. I had some old beat-up bass drum- I covered it with flitter-cloth and then I did the same thing with an old tom-tom that I picked up and a snare drum. I had a very jazzy looking silver flitter looking outfit. I had a little gong that dressed up the stage behind me. It got so that we really looked like we were really professional type players.

It was Flo Whitman's all-girl show at the time and then occasionally they would change and Ralph 'Cookie' Cook and acts like that would come in but usually they were all-girl shows. A lot of strip acts and a lot of novelty acts. I took advantage of the experience, I believe, because we played all types of acts. Not only that, but if somebody in the cast got sick and they needed a few minutes I would go out there and either do a tap dance or a comedy strip. What 'Cookie' Cook used to refer to as "imitations of birds, beasts, and my mother-in-law". We had quite a following with that little band for almost two years.

Mort Lond & His Londoners at "DUTCH'S"

Hank Penny- arm trumpet, Mort Lund- tenor sax and violin, Maurie Lishon- drums, Irv Ruby- piano, Lester Schein- bass, Dorothy London- Mistress of Ceremonies. (Not pictured; Vic Canova- sax.)

 It was the year of the World's Fair and there was a lot of musical action in the Chicago metropolitan area. I was there, as I said, almost two years and got a world of experience and then an opportunity came for me to go on the road with a big band and 'revue playing' theaters. I decided that I would make a change because I wanted to play with a big band and get the experience of playing in theaters acquainting myself with the atmosphere of the theater because by this time I'd decided this was going to be my career.

So I joined Del Coon's Orchestra, who had a big band, good players, and went on a theater tour. It was called a 'Tab Revue' at the time, and the scale, I think, was $35.00 a week on the road. The name of the Revue was "Around The Town With The WBBM Air Theatre". (Featuring acts from radio. Fifteen years later I was on the staff of the WBBM Air Theater. We played theaters around the midwest for several months. In Chicago we ended up playing Christmas week at the Palace Theater. Now imagine there's Maurie Lishon at the Palace Theater.... what's that line? "I made the Palace" "I Played the Palace" it was a wonderful feeling!

Maurie Lishon "playing the palace" with The Del Coon Orchestra ("Around The Town With The WBBM Air Theatre")

GETTING THE GIG AT CHICAGO'S 'ROYALE FROLICS'

Now we're back on the road, and remember I told you that was Christmas week at the Palace. I was with that group until sometime the following March. I was playing little clubs and something came up with Lou Singer, who was the drummer with my brother Hank's band and one of the top to this day- he's passed away, but he's still recognized as one of the greats on the Hollywood scene for the last 30 years or more. Here was the situation.... Lou was leaving Hank's band to join Gus Arnheim's jazz band, which was a big name in those days. Hank had been auditioning every drummer in town, because the shows were very tough. He had about three of four days left on Lou Singer's four week notice and he came to me one day and he said "Hey kid- You play drums, don't you?" I said yes, and he said "You ever play any shows?" I said yeah, and he said "You ever play big ones?" I said "What's the difference? The tempo change at the Royal Frolics is no different than the ones at the Paddock Club!" Well-this was a different situation because the Royal Frolics had the biggest shows in town -even bigger than the Chez Paree in those days.

I had met Janice at the Royal Frolics when I joined the band in 1935 and that year we started going out together. We had some lovely times. I was just crazy about her. We used to go to breakfast dances at Rum Boogie and Swingland on Saturday mornings and we'd go to the park in the afternoon. (We didn't get out of the Royal Frolics til five o'clock in the morning.)

The funny part of it is there was a hard law about fraternization at the Royale Frolics. The band guys were not allowed to fraternize with the girls in the show and we had 20 girls in that show. So what happened was that Dennis Cooney who owned the Royale Frolics felt that Janice and I made a nice couple and never said anything about it or even frowned on the idea that he was breaking his own laws internally.

We developed a lovely relationship and she stayed at the Frolics for four years while all the time that I was at the Grand Hotel during that summer she went to California.

We got married on September the 18th, 1938. We had the wedding in my mother's and father's house and Dennis Cooney who owned the club, (an Irishman) gave Janice away, four Italians held a canopy, and a Rabbi married us. She has been the love of my life; I don't know what I would ever have done all these fifty years... God was good to me when He introduced me to Jan.

The band played seven nights a week, from eight until five in the morning. We had two other alternate dance bands 'cause we were the show band. What happened, the way the shows were laid out, (Duke Yellman was the producer) they did four shows a night, they had five acts, they did three production numbers in each show, and each show had different production numbers and different numbers for the acts, so you know that was a lot of show. A show came in and lasted for six weeks and they played top names. Our scale for the job was 54.00 a week, and for that I had to play timpani, and chimes, and vibraphone or bell parts.

A funny little tidbit about my auditioning for the job.... I was working at a place on the south side with a five-piece band. We worked until 5 o'clock in the morning and Hank said "Come on and audition-You might as well-everybody else in town has." So I said fine, and he said "OK, be here at 2:00 on such and such a night (Two o'clock in the morning, that is) and so I hired a drummer to come in for me at 2:00 on my job. I went downtown to audition for the job. How was he auditioning me? On a DANCE set, which doesn't make sense when it comes to the difference between that and having to play 5 acts and three production numbers. Anyway, I talked to the jazz tenor man on the band, who was very good-a great musician and a writer in those days, by the name of Dean Schaffer I said 'On your jazz choruses, what do you like behind you on drums?' He said "Well, out in Iowa there was a drummer I worked with years ago, he used to play something on a tom-tom back of me with one hand, and I don't know what he did with the other, but it really used to get under me and make me go! So, whatever-" Anyway, we got to playing the set and everything was loud in those days. I see this guy stand up, so I figure if he's standing up he must be playing a jazz tenor solo. Well, I thought of what he told me and I played that beat behind him and when he finished his chorus he turned around and gave me the donut and nodded very intelligently, I thought- obviously he was happy with what I did. So after we got through and got off the bandstand, Hank called me on the side he says "Jesus! You see a guy standing up even if you can't hear, you know he's playing a solo-why dontcha get behind him and PUSH him." I said "Well, it's very funny you should say that, because I asked him what he liked before we played the set and he told me about this beat, and that's exactly what I played for him and he loved it!" He says "Well- the hell with that! Who you gonna satisfy-him or the leader?"

There were no ifs, ands, or buts working for Hank. When he hired me, he said I had to take care of the music library; pick out the old stuff, put in the new stuff. In those days, that's when they were doing remote broadcasts and the song pluggers were always giving you new stuff. I had to do everything but clean up the bandstand and he said one of the clauses was that any time I wasn't doing a job that was up to his expectations or up to what he wanted, he could fire me without any notice.

Henry Lishon and His Orchestra
Front, from left: Lee Davidson, Hal Weber, Bill Scott, Hank Lishon, Ralph Blank, Lee Knight, Les Fulle
Rear, from left: Maurie Lishon, George Marshall, Rudy Faust, Mike Rubin, Len Pitzele, Nate Bold

The jazz quintet from Henry Lishon's Orchestra. Maurie Lishon is on drums, and Mike Rubin is on bass. At this writing, Rubin is the music contractor for 20th Century Fox.

Hank always had the best musicians in town, even though the jobs didn't pay any more, because the guys wanted to play, and in those days that was one of the best jobs in town and one of the highest scales. You didn't get extra for playing shows or anything in those days. In fact, I don't even know if the saxophone players even got doubles. Anyway, that job turned out to be something. Course I had my problems; I had to get some chimes from Roy Knapp and I had to buy some timpani, which I bought from the Chicago Board of Trade band- Joe Kalabza; I still remember that. I invested a lot of money I didn't have, but I paid it off, and the job REALLY was something, because I got more experience there... Funny part; I joined that band on April Fool's day, 1935, and I stayed there for two years with Hank and then we left and Mark Fisher came in, in 1938. Tommy Thomas (a legend) was the drummer.

Henri Lishon and the Selmer Sax Section at Chicago's Stork Club

(L to R) Maurice Campbell, Russ Jones, Henri Lishon, Pete Wandell, Jack Swatek

JOINING THE EDDIE VARZOS ORCHESTRA

I went out and did some clubbing for a while- I went to Texas with Hank's band that summer of '37 and when I came back, I did some free-lancing. Then I joined Eddie Varzos band. He had just closed the Bismarck Hotel and we were playing some hotels and then going to the Grand Hotel on Mackinac Island for the summer of '38.

One of the highlights of that Eddie Varzos band, something for which I am most grateful was the fact that I had the work for a long time, to meet AND work with the great Jose Bethancourt who in my opinion is the greatest marimba player that ever came out of Guatemala.

I've worked with him on and off different places in later years; I worked with him at NBC. Joe was a fantastic player.

That summer at the Grand Hotel at Mackinac Island was a rough one; we had four sessions a day, ALL IN A DIFFERENT PLACE! It was really the hard way, because they had always used two bands there, and Varzos was going to show them that it could be done with one band. We had four different books; we had a regular dance library, we had a gypsy book, we had a classical library for concerts, we had a latin book. It was one of those kind of bands with the fiddle doubles and everything. We had shows to play... it was a really rough job. (I followed Bobby Christian in the band.) But again... it was more experience!

We had a four o'clock session in a tea garden which was down like 300 feet from the hotel, and all steps- we had to carry stuff. Then we had another session at six o'clock in the dining room, where we played concert music. Then we had another one at 7:30 in the lobby which was another concert. Then at nine o'clock we'd go into one of the two big ballrooms, for dancing and a show. So you can see it was a rough job for one guy. (Although Bethancourt helped with some of the stuff besides playing Marimba, thank the Good Lord!)

There's a funny incident- before we went to the Grand Hotel we played the Empire Room in the Schroeder Hotel in Milwaukee. We were doing a broadcast one night and the way we had them lined up, there was a tune called "Say Si Si" or "Par Amigo Mi Voy" in Spanish. There also was a current hit by a local Chicago man, a man by the name of Jack Fascinato called "Sissy". We got these tunes back to back in the broadcast. Evidently when Eddie called the tunes out, he said "SisSY" and "Si Si" so some had lined up "Sissy" and "Si Si", others had "Si Si" and "Sissy". Well, we went on the air and half the band was playing one thing and half the band was playing the other and he kept saying "SisSY" or "Si Si" instead of saying "Par Amigo Mi Voy" which would have solved the problem. So we struggled through two and a half minutes of that and we were on the air in a broadcast. HELP!

I started doing a lot of sub dates and club work around town after we got back in '38 and in the beginning of '39 I joined 'Ramona And Her Men Of Music'. A New York Band, Ramona had just come off of Paul Whiteman's Orchestra. She was a good singer and a fine pianist and she had this all male band and it was a good band. The Rockwell-O'Keefe office was trying to break this band up because it was a bevy of communists who had formed a corporation and the Rockwell-O'Keefe office was stuck with a lot of red shirts and they were making it tough. So the first two replacements in the band were me on drums and a trumpet player the name of Bobby Geyer who later on worked with Woody Herman, Benny Goodman, and bands like that.

"Ramona & Her Music Men", Surf Club, Virginia Beach, June of 1939

So I joined Ramona and I was with her on the road for about ten months. I joined the band in Memphis and I'll never forget... it was a theater. It was a Whiteman alumni duo; Jack Fulton and Ramona were the headliners. We rehearsed the show, and we did the first show. I played my usual style (aggressively) and after the first show I went back and introduced myself to Ramona again, and said "I'm your new drummer.. and I'd like to straighten something out in case there's any feelings, 'cause I know in a couple instances that I took the thing away from you on tempos." She said "Maurie, if that's your name-Thank you very much! I've been a piano player, a singer and an emcee. When I introduce an act and I give a downbeat, I'm with YOU. So thank you for your help and I appreciate it."

I always got along well with leaders. I never ran out of a leader, and I always tried to do the best no matter what a job paid. I always tried to do my best, not $10.00 worth for $10.00, or $20.00 for $20.00 worth.

I stayed on the road with Ramona's band for most of 1939. We played all over the country; a lot of rough jumps and occasionally if we were going to be someplace for more than a day or two or three Jan would meet me for a couple of days and we would enjoy each other's company. It was a pretty rough 8 or 9 months- I was only making about $75.00 a week which was fair money in those days but we had some murderous one-nighters and some characters in the band.

I developed one relationship with a tenor saxophone player in the band by the name of Mack Robbins and Mack passed away acouple of years ago but we had been in contact with each other all those years. He was a wounderful guy and with Mackie and a couple of other names that will appear in this book I developed some wonderful relationships in my lifetime and am proud of some of the fellas I knew and the tremendous talent some of these fellas had. I was VERY lucky, working with people with talent. Another guy that I have kept in contact with all these years out of Ramona's band, who now lives in California, in Carlsbad, LaCosta, Sid Grazzi we are still in contact with each other and he's a wonderful guy. He's been very successful and he's another name that I'm proud to have known.

Now with Ramona's band there was an incident; I told ya we did a lot of one-nighters... We were playing in Vicksburg, Mississippi. We had a noon session the next day in Virginia Beach at the Terrace Club. Now that's a big jump from Vicksburg to Virginia Beach. We had to take a ferry boat on the way there, and on the ferry that we were taking, there were five bands that had all closed the night before. Lou Breese's band, our band, Gray Gordon's band, I think the Hal Kemp band, and Lou Burn or somebody like that. Well, I don't have to tell you what that ferry ride was like. Five bands, comprised of some pretty nutty musicians..... (course that didn't include me, because I was always pretty level headed- you know THAT!)

We had to travel in our own cars in those days because you couldn't make the jumps on the kind of busses they had, there was no plane travel (nobody could afford it). But at about six o'clock in the morning (on that jump from Vicksburg Mississippi to Virginia Beach) I'm on my way and I'm just outside of Chattanooga and it's just turning light. I hear a trumpet playing and I make a turn on a curve and there's one of our cars in a ditch! Hank Jackson, who was one of our trumpet players, bombed out of his mind, is there playing his trumpet. I stopped and asked what happened. He says "Well... we just went in the ditch. We're waiting for somebody to pull us out." So I had to take part of the library- Mackie, Robbins, and Mickey Vena and Sid were with me in my car at the time I believe. So I had to take what I could of the library because when those things happen, and you gotta start at twelve o'clock you gotta start with whatever is there. If the whole band isn't there you still have to start, to fulfill your contract. It's a wild thing to make a curve at six o'clock in the morning and hear a trumpet player in the ditch and it winds up to be one of your own guys.

While we were all in New York with Ramona I was offered a job by Emery Deutsch; the show band at the Paradise Restaurant. I didn't have a New York card, but he said if I came back to New York he would try to help me get a card and offered me the job. Well, I figured I'd go back to Chicago to straighten out some of my business and maybe take a wack at New York. So I went back, but as soon as I got back, things started like crazy for me. I started getting all kinds of calls. I figured as long as I'm keeping busy and making a living, I'll just stay there and see what happens. Finally, I decided to stay.

I worked at the Colony Club with Nat Farber, a Latin band. Nat and I grew up together. He was one of the finest musicians I have ever known. He learned all about Latin music working in the real Latin dives in Chicago and he was really an authentic Latin player. He taught me a lot about Latin- between him and Joe Bethancourt. I had followed a fellow by the name of Willie Rodriquez into the Colony Club. Willie was recognized as one of the greatest Latin players in the country and he had gone back to Puerto Rico or someplace-he was pretty well shot personally... I took his place; I was always following the tough guys it seems. I took his place in the Colony Club. Nat was the musical director of that band; it was remnants of the old Carlos Molina Band. All we did was just play Latin music seven nights a week. I was getting pretty tired of it. When the job came up at Michael Todd's for the off night when they wanted to develop a six-day week for musicians and my brother got the call he asked me if I would take off and play with him becasue he felt more at ease with me on drums I guess. I said "Talk to Nat, and if it's alright with Nat, fine." I wanted to play a big show anyway. We rehearsed the show and I did the show that night. The guy that owned the Colony Club was a real "heavy" in the syndicate by the name of Nick Dean (later one of the fellas that was involved in that multimillion dollar extortion deal with the movie-picture operators Brown and Bioff. We played the show and played the dance after the show and who do I see dancing in front of the bandstand but Nick Dean with his gal (kind of a well-known gal around town). He's looking at me like there's no tomorrow for me. I got home and I got a call from Nat Farber about four o'clock in the morning and he says "Maurie, did you see Mick Dean?" "Yeah." "Well, that's alright but what's worse is he saw you. He came back really stomping for your scalp. So tonight when you come to work, come in at about one minute to eight, come in the back door, and go right up on the bandstand." I did, because he was really out to get me for taking off and going to play at Michael Todd's. It wore off, and everything came out alright. Some months after that, they found his girl friend burned to death; her name was Estelle Carey.

Nat was closer to me than a brother could be for years and I will never forget him. He was a great talent. He was the musical coordinator for Carol Burnett's show when she was on the network for many years and before that he'd been for seven years the musical coordinator with Dinah Shore when she was on for Chevy.

BREAKING THE SEVEN-DAY LAW AT THE MICHAEL TODD THEATER

In 1940 I went to work with Hank's band at Michael Todd's theater cafe. That was Michael Todd senior, THE Michael Todd. He had a place on the North side that had great big shows. The first show that they brought in was called 'Gay New Orleans', from the New York World's Fair. They brought the whole show intact featuring Gypsie Rose Lee. It was a beautiful show, it was a big show, and it was a tough show. Very well produced by top people-this is Josh Logan type of stuff. When this thing came up at Michael Todd's the union wanted to prove that a band could come in one night a week and do a show. All the musicians were playing seven-day-a week jobs and couldn't have a night off. They wanted to take the toughest show in town which was at Mike Todd's, the Gay New Orleans Show, and use that as an example. Well, who'd they pick for the show band but my brother Hank. It was a tremoundous band. We did that show and we really knocked it off. It broke the seven-day law; that's when it first went to six and in later years it went to five. I still have pictures of that band, and a story from Intermezzo (the Chicago Federation of Musician's paper) showing a picture of the band and the personnel and a little bit of a story about the fact that this was the band that broke the seven-day law.

The Michael Todd Theater, where Henry Lishon's Orchestra
(on the left, with Maurie Lishon on drums) broke the seven-day law.

DURING THAT YEAR (1940) I WORKED AT SEVERAL OTHER PLACES, SUCH AS THE "UNCLE TOM'S CABIN IN SWING REVUE" WITH HENRI AT THE STATE-LAKE THEATER

Finally Les Brown's band came in and they were the house show band for a while. We were still doing the off-nights, and we had Joe Sanders on the other bandstand as the dance band. When Les Brown went back to New York we were the house band from then on for a couple of months until we went to work one Wednesday night and found out that the joint had been padlocked! So there we were high and dry, and the next day I got a call from Boyd Raeburn who wanted to know if I could work with him on Monday night at the Chez Paree, that it was an audition. Paul Whiteman had been the house band there and was screwing up the shows something fierce and they were looking for a semi-'name' local band to save money and Boyd had gotten the call. We played the Monday night, the audition worked, and I went into the Chez Paree for six months in the show band with Boyd Raeburn.

The Boyd Raeburn Band, at the "Chez Paree"

I told Boyd when I went in that I wasn't interested in traveling; I didn't want to take the job while it was local and then screw him up when he had to go on the road. In those days we had the broadcasts that built up the audience to support the series of one-nighters on the road. But he said "All right" and the first show we had was with Milton Berle. Boyd Raeburn was not the greatest musician in the world. He had great ideas, he was years ahead of his time in what he heard but he wasn't the greatest instrumentalist. He was a wonderful guy to work for. The funny thing was that they hired Boyd Raeburn to be the house show band when Boyd Raeburn wasn't the greatest show band conductor in the world, it would seem. As it turned out, he had replaced four or five of the men in the band to go into the Chez, to get men who could handle the shows. I was one of them, we had Mike Rubin on bass, we had Howard Davis, a very fine legitimate trumpet player, and John Blount a fine lead alto saxophone player, and we took the shows. He shifted the other men for the dance music, so it worked out all right.

FROM THE JULY 16th, 1941, EDITION OF "VARIETY":

BOYD RAEBURN ORCHESTRA (15), Chez Paree, Chicago: Here is a group which, though consisting mainly of Chicago boys, is new to Chicago cafedom. Making the debut doubly hard is the fact that the band has had to follow name outfits into this spot, and hold up under the pressure of a difficult show and a lot of air time. However, the band is scoring well.

Instrumentation is the standard setup with five brass, four rhythm, four saxes, with Raeburn himself occasionally picking up the fifth sax. Band is flexible, playing the society brand of music or the jump tunes. Proficient, too, in playing for show. Particular credit is owing the drummer, Maurie Lishon, who works with the floor acts every minute.

Outstanding musicianship in the band is perhaps contributed by Emmett Carls on tenor sax, and Mike Rubin on bass, with Hal Derwin, guitarist, turning in a nice job on the vocals. The second trombonist, Ray Thomas, also deserves mention for his arrangements. Raeburn is a friendly guy with an affable personality.

It would be difficult to list all the top show-business personalities Maurie worked with, especially at this stage of his career. Among the stars he backed up were: Eddie Cantor, Ethel Waters, George Jessel, Sophie Tucker, Joe E Lewis, Buddy Clark, Johnny Desmond, Arthur Godfrey, Al Hirt, Joey Bishop, Danny Thomas, Gypsy Rose Lee, Bob Eberly, Vic Damone, and Jimmy Durante.

Jimmy Durante was a comedian who occasionally picked on the drummer. During one show in which Maurie was playing straight man for Durante, suddenly Durante heaved a telephone through one of the drums. There was a tremendous crash that nearly knocked Maurie off his throne.

Maurie-
"It was understood in show business that Durante paid for anything he broke- and he broke plenty!

Cues were always duck soup for me; I never had any problem with cues because so many things are natural. Well, Milton Berle carried his own show- he had eight fellows who called themselves the Ben Yost singers. Ben Yost had about five different groups around the country; this one particularly were called the 'Eight White Guards'; I had worked with them previously at Michael Todd's too. Berle would come out and do a burlesque with these guys and they were dressed like the old king's guardsmen and stuff and he had the comedy outfit on. Milton wanted you to catch everything. "Catch everything, Mr Drummer" was a favorite phrase for vaudeville. Well, as it turned out, with these eight guys (none of them were under six feet- something tall) I couldn't see Berle when he stepped off and he used to say "How would you like to like to walk into the Edgewater Beach Hotel with this outfit on?" Then he would step off and he wanted you to catch it with the bass drum. Well, I couldn't see him. If he had moved his head, but he just moved his legs so I couldn't catch the cue.

He raised hell with Raeburn that the drummer was missing cues. Actually that was the only cue I was missing and it was because I couldn't see it. Finally, after the second or third show Raeburn came back to me and said "Maurie... You're not catching the cues for Berle!" I said "Wait a minute! What I can see I can catch." He said "Well, he's jumping all over me." I said "You tell him if he's got a beef about the drums, talk to me." He said "Don't get hot, don't get excited- see what you can do about it." I went back to Berle's dressing room and introduced myself to him, said I was the drummer, and that the one cue that he's talking about was impossible for me to catch because I couldn't see his body move. "If you move your head forward at the same time you're moving your leg, then I can catch the cue." He said "Well, there's no problem!" "Well, there seems to be with Boyd, 'cause he's all nervous and he need this job bad!" He said "No, I don't mean to cause any problems-You're all right. What'd you say your name was?" "Maurie Lishon" "I know you from someplace." "Probably when you used to come in on the celebrity shows at the old Royal Frolics- I was in the show band there." "I knew you looked familiar! Now I know all about you. I'm glad you're here. Don't worry about a thing-everything is fine." From then on, I could do absolutely no harm with Milton Berle for the next six weeks. He loved me and Mike Rubin and used to send drinks up to us right in the middle of the show.

Berle used to clown with Mike and me a lot. One time in the middle of a show he came up to me, got behind me, grabbed my collar on my shirt, took it around my neck and tore the whole collar off. Then he used it for two or three gags and we went on with the show. After the show he said to come over to his dressing room. So I did and he said "Here- I've got a shirt for you to put on, to wear for the next show." In those days they had collar points that went down about six inches- it was really something to see. I wore a 14 and he wore a 16 1/2. In the middle of the show he started putting me on with the audience-'how do I like the shirt', 'how do they like the shirt that I'm wearing'. He said "Open it up, show 'em the initials. Show 'em who's shirt it is." (Because it had an MB over the pocket.) I opened it up, and he said "Tell 'em who's shirt it is." I said "There it is-MB; My Brother's!" I got a laugh, he got a laugh.

The job at the Chez Paree was very interesting for six months...We played all top acts; the cream of vaudeville and show business played the Chez Paree. I got to play a lot of top acts, and they let a drummer go- a drummer was very important in those shows in those days because they were actually vaudeville acts whether they were in a theater or a night club- it didn't make any difference. It was just a wonderful experience for me and it looked well on my resume (one of which I never had)."

Another interesting thing at the Chez Paree- they brought in an act; her name was Carmen Amaya. She had her whole family with her and they did a flemenco act. Flamenco dancing was very big at that time and she was probably the greatest flamenco dancer in the world and she LOVED me. Backstage she and I would get together and I'd show her some American hoofing steps and she'd show me flamenco steps and it was a wonderful time, I'll never forget it. I was very influenced by the rhythmic impulse that she projected. To me she was one of the most tremendous rhythmic individuals that I ever ran into in my life and in my lifetime I've run into some rhythmic individuals.

List of Available
DRUMMERS' PHOTOGRAPHS

ORMOND DOWNES Kay Kyser	HERMAN KAPP Roger Pryor	HARRY LINDEMAN Freddy Fisher	AUGIE THIELMAN Bob Strong
ROY KNAPP Noted Teacher	BOBBY CHRISTIAN NBC Chicago	LOU SINGER CBS Chicago	JOE CARTZ Tommy Reynolds
GEORGE WETTLING Paul Whiteman	SAM TAYLOR Phil Harris	CHARLIE MASTER Camel Caravan	LYLE SMITH Own Trio
COZY COLE Coomer. Jones	PAUL COLLINS Jack Teagarden	JOHNNY JACOBS Hollywood Studios	MAURIE LISHON Chez Paree, Chicago
BOB WHITE Freddie Martin	RUSS ISAACS Jan Savitt	RED SAUNDERS Own Orchestra	GIL BAER Leonard Kellar
SID CATLETT Louie Armstrong	FRANK FLYNN Ted Flo Rito	FRANK RULLO NBC Chicago	REEF McGARVEY Toronto, Canada
BEN POLLACK Own Orchestra	ALLEN KIMMEY CBS Chicago	BOB SPANGLER Vincent Lopez	BUDDY BURTON Milt Herth
EDDIE SHEA Kay Kyser	LILLIAN SINGER Ina Ray Hutton	BUD MOORE San Francisco Studios	
RALPH SMITH NBC Chicago	MURRAY GAER Abe Lyman	ABE GAER Little Jack Little	HARRY BUDDINGER NBC Chicago

Ludwig & Ludwig, Inc.
1101 BEARDSLEY AVE.   ELKHART, INDIANA

114-L-AR

These Ludwig & Ludwig players did not get paid for their endorsements. They did not even get free equipment or big discounts. Maurie says "We were just grateful for the exposure! It was considered an honor to have a major manufacturer use your photo for promotional purposes."

    After I left the Chez, I went into the Pump Room with the Jerry Shelton Orchestra. Jerry Shelton had been musical director for "Veloz and Yolanda", recognized at that time as the world's greatest dance team. This was a terrific group-it was an eight piece band but we had great arrangements and great players. Again, Mike Rubin was in that band, and Freddy Aune, Harry Hynda was a great piano player, and Eddie Pripps, Buddy Berkshire.

    We did some recordings with Buddy Clark at the time. We stayed there about six months. It was one of the better jobs in town, and the band was sensational- it was about 20 years ahead of it's time. Most of our book was written by Tony Iovello who wound up as the musical director/conductor/arranger for Mario Lanza.

    We're at about 1940 now, and in between when I wasn't working a steady job I was doing club dates with the better leaders around town-mostly show jobs, and it was pretty weird in those days; a class-A job was three hours for ten dollars and you didn't get paid extra for a show. You paid 4% tax, so if the job was a three-hour job, you took home $9.60. The class-B jobs were 3 1/2 hours for $8.00, with a 2% tax, so you wound up with $7.84. Many a time I would play a show at a Class-B and drive 40 miles to play a show with Herby Mintz or Al Marny and the job would pay $7.84. The following day on a Saturday night at one of the downtown hotels that same show, three hours for $9.60.

    I went to work at Colosimos and that was the year, on November 22, 1941, Janice gave birth to our beloved Chuck. We were thrilled to have a son; he was something we were very proud of. Two weeks after he was born, on December 7th, 1941, was the day that the Japs bombed Pearl Harbor. You can imagine our feelings with a newborn son. Chuck was a very important part of our lives and we did what we could. It was about that time that we moved into Spalding Ave where my folks had an apartment- they were at the back of the court and we were in the front of the court. My mother and dad were crazy about Chuck.

    In 1942 the Hal Kemp band was one of the hottest bands in the country. Hal Kemp was killed in an automobile accident and the band was coming into the Blackhawk Cafe which was THE spot for a dance band to be, because they had the best radio broadcast outlet in the country. They played only the name bands and the name bands wanted to play there because they wanted that broadcast. They were coming in in September and I'm high and dry around the first of June thinking I'm going to get stuck playing the country clubs all summer. But as it turned out I was offered the job to go in the Blackhawk with them in September. Now I had to fill in July and August.

Just about that time, I got a call from my dear friend Sol Wagner who told me that the leader of the band at the Rialto Theater (which was a big burlesque house) wanted to see me. I went down to see him and he explained to me that his drummer (that band had been there for years; it was a closed, tight island, burlesque was in those days) was going away on a six week vacation, would I want to come in and fill in the six weeks. I figured well that's perfect to take me through the summer although I'd never played a burlesque theater. I'd played strip acts and a lot of strip joints but I'd never actually been in burlesque theater. I went in and rehearsed the first show, and played the show which went smooth as silk. After the show I went up to the leader and says "Is there anything you want that you're not getting, or anything that you're getting that you don't want? 'Cause I'm pretty flexible." He says "Maurie, you're doing fine." I was following another tough guy because Ray Lannon had a tremendous show reputation.

At the end of the second week we're in on Friday at seven or eight o'clock rehearsing the new show, we did the show, and after the show Abe said he wanted to talk to me. (Abe Merer was the leader- wonderful man.) He said the owner of the theater had come back and talked to him; he was very impressed with the new drummer and he wanted to know if he could hire me permanently. I wasn't one to go take anybody's job; I told him I wasn't sure, I'd have to check it out about taking the job steady. I discussed it with Jan and we realized that was the best-paying theater job in Chicago because it was in two four-hour shifts and the scale turned out to be even higher than the Chicago theater unless the Chicago theater had a heavy show where the guys were doing six shows a day. I accepted the job, and I stayed there until November of 1943; almost two years.

INTO THE ARMY

Then came the draft call. I'd had Colitis attacks off and on every few months from nerves so when my draft call came up, Abe said "Don't worry about it- you won't last a week, they won't even take ya." They weren't taking men over 26 and they weren't taking fathers. I was 29 and Chuck was going on three. Well, they took me and I was requisitioned for a band up in Detroit with Carmen Dello. Abe told me "Look, you won't be there very long. They'll let you out. So hire somebody to work for you til you get out and if you come back on Monday and you want to come back into the pit on Tuesday, it's your job." I said "No, YOU better hire somebody." He hired somebody, and I figured the only way to get out of the army was to get my spastic colon to kick up. I started drinking all the bad booze and eating all the bad food I could get my hands on to kick it up. I stayed in the army for two years and, knock on wood, I never had any Colitis problems since. So join the army if you want to get rid of your Colitis.

I was requisitioned for the band in Detroit but at the same time I'd had a letter from Eddie Peabody requesting that I try to come up to Great Lakes (Naval Base) and see if they could use me in ship's company there. They had a lot of great players at that Great Lakes.

I wound up in Detroit and I was there for about six months and then the Sixth Service Command rebuilt the Army radio unit at Ft Sheridan to be the official band for the Sixth Service Command. I was requisitioned for that band. We had some fine players, and we had the two finest singers in America at the time-Buddy Clark and Bob Eberly. Wayne King was our commanding officer on our concerts and he left a lot to be desired, but he was a Major, and he was the boss, and that's the way it was. I was first chair on everything as a result of which I was playing 15 and 18 hours a day because there was only one other drummer there. Then in the radio unit whatever string players were available to help in percussion, that's what I had to contend with.

They had a big contest shortly after I got to Ft Sheridan to see what was the best Armed Services dance band in the continental United States. The judges were Les Brown, Benny Goodman, and Woody Herman. As if we didn't have enough work to do, we won that thing, which meant a lot more work and we made a lot of V-discs and things. We had some very good men in that band.

GRANT PARK BANDSHELL, 1944   344th A.S.F. DANCE BAND

We did Grant Park concerts during the summer with combining three bands out of the local army units. I was in charge of that... I had to play a dance someplace every single night not counting all of the regular G.I. things that we had to do, and they traveled us all over the Sixth Service Command. I was a little hard to get along with because I was thirty years old & I felt that a younger man should have been doing what I was doing. I stayed in the Army and got out almost 2 years to the day.

The closest I came be being a casualty was when we marched in an "E" award ceremony at the Dow Chemical Plant in Midland, Michigan. Trombone player Tommy Shepherd accidentally stepped on a button that turned on a shower used to decontaminate the chemical workers. The dousing caused the sousaphone player to swing around abruptly to avoid the shower and his big horn hit me. It knocked me backwards and the bandsmen fell like flies.

OUT OF THE ARMY AND ON THE AIR!

I got out on a Monday night, and I never went back to the theater job... I wanted to do bigger and better things. Sure enough, two days after I was out I got my first call to sub at ABC. I went up there, and Rex Maupin was the musical director and Harry Kogen was the assistant and we did back-to-back shows. I lot of the guys that were in the band were friends of mine; they were cueing me on tempos and things like that and if I say so myself I came out pretty well. That started me subbing and the first thing I knew I was getting all the calls for all of the radio station subs. This was just wonderful, because I came out of the army at 72.00 a month for two years; you don't go very far.

Jan had been working her brains out as a filing clerk at 1st National Bank and she was dumping Chuckie off at a day-nursery on her way to work. We had kept our $40.00 a month apartment and the first thing we did every week was to put that 10.00 aside for the rent. Janice was something else- a real trouper if there ever was one and I'm so proud of everything she has done all of our married lives. After subbing at all the stations I finally got a call from Caesar Petrillo to come on the staff at CBS WBBM. (In the Wrigley building in those days.) I took the job and the only show that I had was a thing called the 'Adventurer's Club', a dramatic show, on Saturday morning on the full network.

The show was a blood and gutsy thing; it was mostly dramatizations of occurences in the lives of the members of the 'Adventurer's Club'. There was just a Hammond organist, myself, two sound men, and a very heavy pro cast. (There were two other drummers, Al Kimmey and Hubert Anderson.) Mike Wallace was one of the steadies on that in those days, and Cliff Norton who later went on to big network things. I made my own percussion parts off of the organ parts. The show was on for a year and a half. When the show went off, there I was sittin there as the third man with no shows and I was on sustaining making 125.00 a week and I wasn't playing. I wasn't making any money nor was I playing. I went to Caesar Petrillo and asked him if I could get out. It wasn't easy to quit Caesar Petrillo. I told him I could make it on the outside. He insisted that he wanted to keep me because one of these days they were going to get a television channel and he wanted me around when that happened. I said "Let me out, and we'll talk when the time comes." He said "Well, will you leave your big stuff here?" That was a godsend for me because I had no place to leave it anyway.

So I went out, and when I went out into the open market, that's when TV broke. WGN, ABC (which was WENR in those days), and NBC all got their TV channels at approximately the same time. Their staff radio schedules were full up, so they needed outside men on some of the stuff and I was the first call on drums on all of them.

MAURIE WITH ONE OF THE FIRST TELEVISION CAMERAS IN CHICAGO. (Wooden Tripod!)

I came out of the army in hock up to my neck, and I was hungry. I didn't turn anything down. Between swings at the theaters, television shows, recordings and club dates, I was doing two and three dates a day. As I said, I was hungry and we really needed the money. I did that for about 10 or 11 months and then finally Jan said "Maurie, this is too much. You're going to have to sit yourself down, you're killing yourself." So I went back on staff at WBBM. I was caught in the switches working at WGN for Bob Trendler, working for Joe Galichio and NBC, working for Rex Maupin at ABC, Caesar Petrillo at WBBM-CBS; all on a substitute basis.

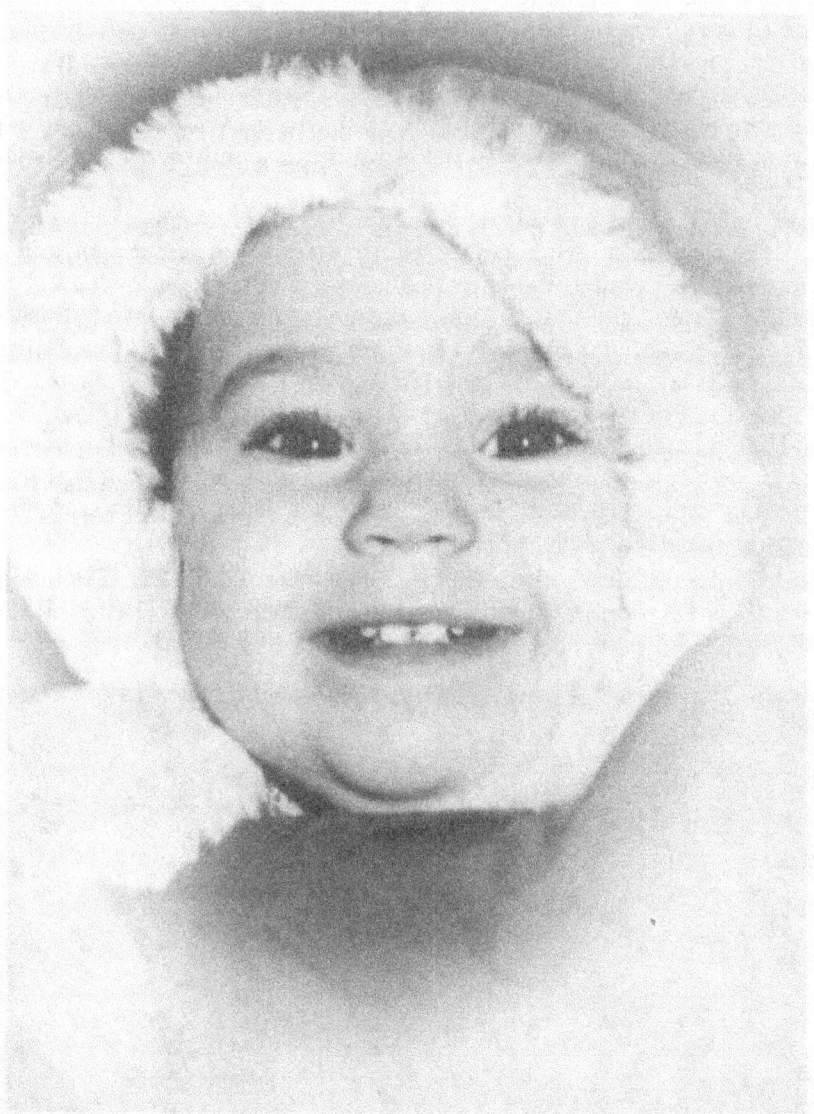

SUZANNE LISHON WAS BORN ON OCTOBER 24, 1947

The Lishon's started to build a house about this time, and their 3rd child, Marty, was born on January 22, 1951

With two young children and a new house, Maurie and Jan were barely making ends meet. It just wasn't possible for them to go in with Maurie's three brothers (as originally planned) on opening a music store. The other three went ahead with the plan, opening the store on the ground floor of the Musician's Union Building around 1949. Hank (AKA Henri, Henry, the bandleader) and Ruben (a judge) invested in the store which Jack Lishon operated. They opened up with a stock not only of musical instruments, but also printed music and records. They discovered very quickly that the tremendous walk-in traffic generated by the offices of the telephone company across the street made the record department the real profit center of the store. With records selling so fast, it didn't make sense to even stock musical instruments, so the store soon became a record store. Eventually Jack sold out in order to move to California to pursue a career in the record business.

The Selmer Company introduced their 'Crowell' bass drum pedal at Lishon's music around 1949. Maurie and Jack Lishon were on hand (see autographs on picture), as were Roy Knapp and his son Don, Bob Tilles, and Bobby Christian.

At WGN, something came up with Roy Graham who was the staff drummer; he got his notice. Bobby Christian got his notice at NBC. Somebody else got their notice at another station where I was working, I don't remember who that was. Everybody downtown is looking at me like I'm undermining everybody's jobs, which was ridiculous because most of those guys could play rings around me anyway. They weren't there because they were good looking-they were all great players. Bobby Christian, Frankie Rullo, Roy Graham, Anderson; all great players.

I got a call from Caesar Petrillo to come back on staff. I had determined that I was not going to be on a staff where I was the third luxury man on a luxury chair so that if something came up that's the first man that gets lopped off. I told that to Caesar Petrillo on the phone and he got very indignant and hung up after I made an appointment to see him the following Wednesday. About five minutes later I got a call from a music-business friend (Saul Wagner), who bawled the hell out of me because I had turned Caesar down. I said I didn't turn him down. He said "HE says you did!" I also got a call from Joe Galichio wanting me to come on staff at NBC because Christian had just been let go. I told him that I had promised Caesar that if I went back on a staff job that I would give him the first preference. As it turned out, I went back on staff at CBS-WBBM.

36

In those days if you were on a job that was five days a week, you were frozen. You couldn't do anything else outside except commercial recording. You couldn't do transcriptions, you couldn't do club dates. So there I was, frozen. Bob Trendler over at WGN liked my work so I get a call one day (we were still in the Wrigley Building); there was going to be a television series called the Miss U.S. TV contest. They were having contests in four major locales in the country for thirteen weeks and of the thirteen weeks they would go through processes of elimination and in the thirteenth week the finals were going to be at WGN. This was in conjunction with the railroad fair in those days. I said to Bob "I'm frozen- how can I do a show here with you if I'm on the staff at WBBM?" He said "Don't worry about it." I said "The first time the camera hits the band and Caesar see me in the band, I'll be fired!" "Number one, we'll tell production not to shoot the band at all. It's strictly like a pit band setup; nobody will see you and if something DOES come up, I'll straighten it out with Caesar." "Well-you give me your word on that, I'll take it." I did it for 13 weeks; I'm on the staff at WBBM and working thirteen weeks of shows at WGN which is unheard of.

On the final date of the last show of the finals to pick Miss U.S. TV after all the others had been eliminated, and I was the only sub in the band because the staff was pretty well tied up with other shows. We're rehearsing the show and I'm looking at this one gal and I said to the guys in the band "You see that girl? I don't know who she is, I don't know what she does, or how well she does what she does, but that's got to be Miss U.S. TV. Hands down." This gal came out, she was gorgeous, she was dressed in a lovely white gown, and she did a tremendous arrangment of 'Love Is Where You Find It' and we really kicked the hell out of it. She won, hands down. She was as good as they come. Her name was Edie Adams, and she was something.

Another time I tried taking an outside gig while I was frozen didn't turn out so well.... Davey Tough was playing for Mugsy Spanier at the Blue Note. Davey got sick and they had to have a substitute. I agreed to take the job, which was supposed to pay $30.00, even though I was frozen and Mugsy knew it. I played the job, and spent $10.00 during the evening at the bar. I got pinched for speeding on the way home (trying to get home fast to catch as much sleep as possible before getting to the studio the next morning), which cost me another $10.00. The worst part of the whole thing was that I never got the $30.00! There was nothing I could do-I couldn't go to the union about not getting paid, because I was supposed to be frozen. Bobby Christian had come on staff with us at WBBM. He was on the morning shows with a small group and I was with the big orchestra on the night shift but we had nothing to play except one commercial. That commercial went off, so I was back on sustaining making 140.00 a week. Bobby Christian decided to leave to go back to New York to work with Paul Whiteman at ABC and Bob Tilles came in and took his place on the morning shift with the 4 or 5 piece group.

I took my vacation and when I came back from vacation and went in, Caesar Petrillo was there waiting for me. He told me not to touch any doubles; that the economy department had gone to work on the music department and they were cutting back on money. I said "Well, who's the first man around here?" "Well, you are." "Well, Bobby Tilles is doing the morning shift and I don't want to be a bad guy, but if I'm the first man and there's a commercial shift, I think I should be on it."

Now in those days you had to give or get an eight-weeks notice if you were going to get fired or quit. I told Caesar that if I was the first man I should be getting the commercial shift or the only alternative was to give me eight weeks notice or to give Bobby Tilles his two-week sustaining notice. (In order to take a man off a commercial you had to give him two weeks notice.) He said "See me at the end of the week." At the end of the week I finally got to corner him, because he'd been ducking me, and I said "What's happening, Caesar? You want to give me my notice?" He said "No. We've got 'Life With Luigi' coming in for three weeks and I have to conduct it." (That was a show on with J Carroll Nash on the network at the time.) "And I want you to do it with me. You'll be on commercial for that three weeks and in the interim I can give Bobby his sustaining notice and then you'll go on the morning shift."

It was about at that time that the union had just signed a new five-year contract with the radio and television stations and we had 45 men on staff at those stations at the time. The way the new contract read, they were going to knock off five men at the end of the first year, five men at the end of the second year, no men the third year, five men the fourth year, five men the fifth year, which would have brought the staffs down to 25-man staffs at the end of five years. Seeing the handwriting on the wall, Caesar Petrillo, who was a great administrator (he had to be with 45 prima donna's on his hands, believe me) figured he'd better do something because there were fewer shows to do and more men to pay. He decided to organize out of the big orchestra personnel one band that could do most of the work. So he organized out of that band an eight-piece band comprised of Harold Kartun on piano, Skip Nelson on bass, I was on drums, Joe Rumoro on guitar, Porky Panico on trumpet, Paul Seversen on trombone, Dick Cutliffe on the woodwinds, and Don Orlando on accordian. They put this band together and we proceeded to do all the shows. Before that, when they were using four and five man groups on morning radio, it was catch as catch can.

The eight of us did ALL the shows; the other 17 on staff came and picked up their checks. They never had to blow a note cause there was nothing to play except on the rare occasion they'd come in for something or maybe even only a rehearsal. We covered everything that came out of that station live for several years with that eight-piece band. They STILL talk about that band!

THE 8-PIECE WBBM BAND (left to Right) Skip Nelson-Bass, Maurie Lishon-Drums, Porky Panico-Trumpet, Paul Severson-Trombone, Dick Cunliffe-Reeds, Joe Rumoro-Guitar, Don Orlando-Accordian, Harold Kartun-Piano

That band turned out to be the talk of the town. We were on that morning shift for many, many years. The musicianship, the feeling, the comraderie, the respect for each other is something I have never been a part of or seen anything equal to in all my years in the music business. (And we're talking about seven decades in the music business.)

That eight-piece band was the most unbelievable group of musicians playing together. The sounds that we made were just unbelievable. There was one stretch when we were doing so many shows -we were doing seven shows a day, five days a week!- Prestige clients lined up all the time for air time for sponsorship. That band could play anything and play it right now.

To begin with, Don Orlando was an absolute genius. He was so far ahead of everybody in playing the accordian so it didn't sound like an "A-chord-deen" that it was unbelievable. As far as playing jazz, the guy was a genius. A guy like Art VanDamme who's an international star used to come in the studio every once and a while in the morning and stay in the control booth, look out at Don Orlando, shake his head, and say "You son of a bitch!" in admiration.

A singer like Nancy Wilson might be on a record tour... she'd come in and give us an arrangement that was written originally for eighteen men and took four and a half minutes. We're down to what we have to do for her has to be done in a 2 1/2 minute arrangement. So we have to do the cuts, we have to know how to change the voicing because, we didn't have seven or eight brass and five saxophones. So what we would do during the one-minute transcriptions that were prevalent on the show, we would talk over the cuts and know what the timings were, and Don Orlando would block the harmony parts for the missing brass or saxophones because we had the lead instruments. It would come out sounding like a fifteen or eighteen piece band. The tempos were up to me, the cuts and the harmonizations were up to the rest of the guys.

We had a forty hour week, and out of the forty hours we could play twenty-five. We'd played all of these shows for all those years and came in at seven o'clock ON THE AIR- we didn't come in and rehearse and then go on the air. We were in that studio until ten o'clock every morning doing all those broadcasts and then we'd have our first 1/2 hour off. We'd get breakfast for half an hour, come back up and set up the books for the next day.

BOARDING FOR THE CBS AFFILIATE SHOW
CBS flew the entire crew (the band, the singers, the MC) to New York where simulated broadcasts were performed to the midwest market buyers. (1959) Note the original Wrigley's Doublemint twins, the Boyd Sisters.

The 'Double Your Pleasure' commercials for Wrigley that are on even today and have been for years- we did those the first two years they were in the can. That was something that was done everyday- we'd do a couple five-minute things here, five-minute things there for Doublemint.

The charts and the head arrangments were purposefully tough to keep us on our toes, and it did keep us on our toes. After we'd been on the air for some years, Caesar Petrillo decided to rig up another eight-piece group just like ours with the same instrumentation and use our book. They tried it several different times but they could never get the same sound we got because the book was written for the individuals in that band. (That's no reflection on the other musicians who tried to play that book, they were all excellent musicians. It just never came together like the eight of us gelled as a unit.

We had excellent singers; we had Bob Vegas, Billy Leach, Bill Lawrence who had been on the Godfrey show, we had Carol March (who to this day is a great singer), Ginny Patton, Connie Mitchell. We had three male singers and three female singers, so they had great diversification of programming with the individual vocals plus duets, trios, and quartet things that they worked out...

Lots of times (you know what the weather's like in Chicago) when we'd have blizzards or snowstorms or there'd be automobile problems with some of the people.... Many's the time we went on the air with three, four and five people until everybody got there and showed up, to continue the programming. It was one of the feathers in our caps that we were able to produce all those years under ANY conditions.

When television first broke, we were still in the Wrigley building for our main studios and we had no television studio facilities so CBS had leased the Garrick Theatre downtown for the television performances and television shows. We used to have meetings to come up with ideas, because they were starting from scratch and nobody knew what was going to go. Television was all live; there was no way you could do anything on tape-there was no such thing at the time.

We used to do all of our morning shows and rehearse, then jump in a cab because the end of our eight hour shift was around two o'clock in the afternoon. We would jump in a cab, go to the Garrick Theater and do a television show at noon, come back and have to do one afternoon show. Usually it was with Jim Conway or somebody.

When they needed another minute or minute and a half or two minutes, Phil Bondelli who was the producer would come over and say "Maurie (or Porkie or Joey or Hal) what have ya got for a filler? We used to do all kinds of schtick. Some of them were funny. I remember there was a very popular tune called 'The Man With The Raincoat'. We had a singer by the name of Betty Chappel who had been on the Garroway show at NBC. Billy Leach used to refer to her as Mary Magdalene at the cross because she over-emoted when she was doing a ballad-especially the broken heart stuff. Anyway- she was doing 'The Man With The Raincoat' and before we went on the air Phil Bondelli came over to me and he said "Maurie- if we need some time, there's a raincoat back there that'll fit you. There's also a prop which Joe will show you when we get back there later on that I'll want you to handle, tell you what to do with it." What they were going to do if they needed time was, there was a big prop tree there that she was singing in front of. What I was supposed to do was put this raincoat on and if there was enough time (like 30 seconds) step out holding what turned out to be a fishing pole with something at the end dangling, wrapped in paper, which turned out to be a regular live fish.

I know nothing about fishing or fishing poles, but what I was to do was to step out from the screen area until they went to black. I got the cue because the drums were out on the retard anyway so I had time to do this. I grabbed the pole and I started to step out from behind the tree and as I did I was holding the rod, the line and the fish with one hand. As I stepped out I let go of the line and the fish started to swing out. I'm reaching out there grabbing for the fish and trying to get it under control while I'm trying to walk out; the place was up for grabs until we went to black. For weeks and weeks Betty Chappel was mad at the whole cast because she thought we were really putting her on. To tell the truth we WERE putting her on. She was a nice kid and as I look back it was a nice memory.

Another incident at the Garrick Theater involved a tune by Raymond Scott called "Mountain High, Valley Low". It was decided that Dick Cunliffe (about 6' tall, 220 lbs), and I (little guy), and Billy Leach (a normal individual) were to be dressed in Mandarin costumes. The way they were going to do this, it opened with a picture of a Chinese pagoda and as they dollied out they dollied into the picture of the three of us in the Mandarin costumes. Billy Leach, me in the middle, and Dick Culiffe on the end. The whole thing was staged in such a way that I had a Chinese cymbal on a stand in front of me, Chinese gong behind me, and a pair of finger cymbals on one hand. This whole arrangement (and it was gorgeous-it was a beautiful tune) consisted of finger cymbal, chinese cymbal, gong, and arpeggios on flute. Shing, Bing, Bong... biddlediddledeedleiddleay.... And with that background, he sang "Mountain High, Valley Low" and it was very effective. The thing ran about two and a half minutes and as we're getting down to two minutes, we're starting to get the stretch from the stage director-they want more time. What are you gonna do except keep repeating that thing? So I said to the guys "Keep repeating- it's a stretch." Finally we're getting the 20-second countdown. When I know there's about ten seconds to go, I whispered under my breath "I'll take it." I stepped forward, I hit the finger cymbals, reached back and hit the cymbal, and then reached back and hit the Chinese gong, and then I raised one hand and I said (in Yiddish accented lilting voice) "Once a Yankee, always a yankeee..." as I hit the gong we went to black and the theater broke up.

We did a TV show Monday through Friday at noon called 'Luncheon With Billy' featuring Billy Leach, which also featured some of the swingers on the morning shift. The show opened up with a menu; all it said on the outside was 'Luncheon With Billy'. As the camera dollied out, you see Billy Leach sitting at this table, and he's looking at this menu. Another camera picks it up from a another view, and you still see part of Billy Leach's body and part of the menu and his feet, his legs on the floor. Then a hand reaches in with a pitcher of water... (the table was set very nicely with silver and goblets) and spills some water into the goblet. A fellow by the name of Dick Orkin who much later became very big in Chicago television, was working his first show with us as floor director and he was the guy that was going to pour the water into the goblet. When he reached in his hand was shaking something terrible becasue he was nervous as hell. As his hand shook, some of the ice cubes fell out of the pitcher into the goblet and broke the glass. The water all went into Billy Leach's crotch which was on camera. All you could see was that water and his crotch and his legs shaking! When we saw that on the monitor you can imagine what happened- there was hell to pay! But live television was live television- we couldn't do it over.

The days of live television were very exciting, and you had to know what you were doing. You weren't fooling around with nickels and dimes- it was expensive.

That eleven months that I was out of the station the first time when TV broke I was doing all of the television shows with all of the staff bands and all of the stations when it first broke and I know what I was up against. Experience was a tremendous, tremendous help to me. God was good to me- I'll never forget the opportunities that I had because of the experience that I had and what I was able to do. There's nothing like live television and to this day you'd be amazed at the difference in the feeling of the artists, the performers when they're doing something live as against when they're doing something that if they goof they can do it over again.

ANOTHER LIVE BROADCAST GIG FOR THE ABC STAFF ORCHESTRA IN 1948- "THE SUPER CIRCUS"

The poolside broadcasts from the home of personality Mal Bellairs featured the entire A.M. lineup and became an annual affair. One year an acoustic peculiarity caused a large section of a rock wall along the far side of the yard to collapse.

On the cutting edge of recording technology......

Jack Rael was an old friend of mine who was originally a saxophone player from Milwaukee. He became road manager for a big band. He came over to my house one day and said "I want you to hear something!" He played this dub for me, of a gal he had heard in Oklahoma City. He had tied her up into a 50-50 contract and was planning to make her a star. "I'm going to quit playing saxophone, I'm going to concentrate all of my efforts on working on making this girl a star. I'm going to have to take about 20 pounds off of her, and Janice is going to have to show us how to put makeup on her... She's kind of a hillbilly, but she's going to be a great talent!" Jan showed her how to put makeup on, Jack knocked off 20 pounds, and I helped them get her a job on the staff at WBBM (later on, on Breakfast Club). The girl's name was Clara Ann Fowler, whom most people know better as Patti Page.

We did the first recording sessions for Patti in Chicago. One of the tunes was "With My Eyes Wide Open, I'm Dreaming" with the 4-part harmony-all four parts being sung by her. We didn't have any click tracks or anything in those days- we had to make all four cuts even (tempo wise, and phrasing-wise) and that was the first multi-voice recording that was ever made. I pioneered with that, too.

Once we had cut that side, we had to do something for the B side to turn the record out so we recorded some blues. We just called it Oklahoma Blues because that's where she was from. You listen to that if you ever get a chance; you won't believe how GREAT Patti Page sang blues. It's a shame that she went strictly over to the commercial side because people would have liked some of the other things that she did. (Not that it was a mistake- hardly! You should know what a big star she became singing the things that she did, but Jack was the one that picked all that stuff and he obviously knew what he was doing. Hell of a guy, Jack Rael and a hell of a girl, Patti Page..

In 1954 the Pentron Corporation came up with an idea and they called seven of us in. There was Chubby Jackson, Porky Panico, George Jean, Mike Simpson, Caesar Giovannini, Bob Tilles, and myself. They called us in to make a demo recording one day, and the next day the NAMM show opened and they had it on demonstration so you could go in there and hear each instrument out of individual speakers. Then you could hear the total picture of it monitored into a 1/4" tape. I received a letter from the Pentron Corporation which reads as follows: (dated May 14, 1954) Dear Maurice; I wish to express my personal thanks for the cooperation extended during our recent recording session. We feel that you have pioneered with us in creating a new concept of sound reproduction. I'm sure you'll be interested in hearing this reproduction with the proper speaker components and therefore I am extending to you my personal invitation to visit the Conrad Hilton as my guest.

This was the FIRST recording that was ever done where the individual musicians were recorded on more than four individual tracks.

You Won't Believe Your Ears!

THE ALL-ELECTRONIC ORCHESTRA

a fantastic stereophonic production

Every Half Hour, 10 a.m. to 6:00 p.m.

Suite 521A
ELECTRONIC PARTS SHOW
MAY 17-20, 1954
CONRAD HILTON HOTEL

presented by

THE PENTRON CORPORATION

and

UNIVERSITY LOUDSPEAKERS, INC.

Sounds

Conductor and Arranger . . . . DAVID CARROLL
MUSICAL DIRECTOR, MERCURY RECORD CORP.

MUSICIANS

Chubby Jackson	Bass
Porky Panico	Trumpet
George Jean	Trombone
Mike Simpson	Saxophone
Caesar Giovannini	Piano
Bob Tilles	Percussion
Morrie Lishon	Percussion

RECORDING SUPERVISION:
Bill Putnam, President
Universal Recording Co.
Chicago, Illinois

Program

MAMBO NO. 5

SOUTH

MAMBO JOMBO

UNIVERSITY STOMP

DYNA CORD JUMP

MOOD INDIGO

The Fabulous Dynacord Story

Until the development of the Dynacord Professional Tape Recorder, the recording of more than 4 separate channels on ¼ inch magnetic tape was considered impossible.

Now, Dynacord offers *six* separate channels of high fidelity recording made on ¼ *inch tape* . . . truly an engineering triumph! From the explosive attack of the trumpet to the lyrical expression of the clarinet, the subtle and rich contrasts are yours to enjoy—the most dynamic sound you have ever heard.

Six University Laudspeaker Systems are used for the All-Electronic Orchestra, each designed to give full range to the particular instrument it reproduces. Thus, each recorded channel is played back through its own speaker system — the perfectly matched pair!

The result is a startling "presence." A new sound you will long remember . . . the utimate in stereophonic sound recording and reproduction.

UNIVERSITY LOUDSPEAKERS, INC.
80 S. KENISCO AVE.,
WHITE PLAINS, NEW YORK

THE PENTRON CORPORATION
221 E. CULLERTON ST., DEPT. JN-5
CHICAGO 16, ILLINOIS

Chapter Three
Janice Rogers-Lishon

Jan-
"I was raised in New Rochelle, New York, by my grandparents, who were my mother's father and mother. They took me when I was six months old. I went to school in New Rochelle up until the time I was 13. At that time my grandparents had reverses and I had to go to work. I wasn't really equipped to do anything but dance, so I prevailed on one of my friends in town who had been in Broadway shows to take me to New York to calls.

I was not quite 14 when I got a job and started dancing around. For many years I danced around New York, working my way up to some very well-known places. I also did a few shorts for Warner Brothers.

In 1934 I wound up going to Chicago for what was supposed to be six weeks. I was dancing in a review at the Royale Frolics. We had people like Joe E Lewis, Dolly Kaye, Sid Tormack and the Reese Brothers and Tracy Gale and Leonard, etc; they were all big name acts that worked night clubs. We had-Picture 19 -16 dancers and 8 showgirls. Maurie Lishon was playing in the show band (there were two other bands there to augment; used for certain specialty numbers and dance sets).

After the first year at the Frolics I went out to California where I worked at 20th Century and MGM a little bit. I worked on a movie called 'Mr Broadway' with Ed Sullivan and 'Pigskin Parade' (featuring Judy Garland). I was in California only for the summer, then went back to Chicago. They changed the show every six weeks. At the end of four weeks, we'd move into rehearsing a new show, which would be opening in two weeks. As I mentioned, I was originally supposed to be in Chicago for six weeks. At the end of four weeks the boss and the producer came down and said "We'd like for you to stay for another show." I said "But you PROMISED I could go back to New York!" (I didn't want to be out of New York!) They told me they really wanted me to stay and offered to pay my fare back to New York when it was time to return. That went on for four years.

ROYALE FROLICS PRODUCTION NUMBERS

(above) Janice on left
(below) Janice bottom row, 3rd from left

Maurie-
   "The production numbers at the Frolics were really something! The sets, the costumes- it was a tremendously expensive undertaking. They always took great pains to make things authentic; they'd bring in a tennis coach for numbers where the girls were working with tennis racquets, etc.
   When the Prince of Wales vacated the throne with Wally Simpson, we did a coronation number where between the three bands there were seven trumpets. They brought in a trumpet teacher to teach the girls how to play a fanfare. I don't know how many weeks they worked on that, but with the girls doing that and the seven trumpets from the three bands, it really sounded like a coronation!" (below- Janice bottom left. above- Janice 2nd from left.)

Jan stopped dancing shortly after she and Maurie got married, though she was later called upon to share her expertise....

Jan-
"Like most parents with children in school, I wanted to help out where I could. I volunteered for PTA and different things... The school started up an after-school program called 'Lighted Schoolhouse'. I got called by the Board of Education to come downtown. I thought "Oh my God! One of my kids really DID something!" When I g there, they said they wanted me to take the dance program for 'Lighted Schoolhouse'. I was stunned, and told them "You don't know anything about me! Why would you want me to come in to teach a dance program? I was a chorus girl! I don't have a teacher's degree." They said "We know all about you. We know your qualifications, and we want you."

I kept resisting.. "Why don't you go to one of the Astaire Studios and get somebody...."

"No, we want you. We can't open this program unless you agree to take it. The gym teacher will show you the format and what's expected."

"I don't know if my husband will let me do this.. I have two little ones who wouldn't be elibible for this program."

"Oh you can bring them."

"But I'd have to hire a baby-sitter at school- I don't know if my husband would let me do this..."

"Well, it's a paid job!"

I talked it over with Maurie, who told me "Take it! You might have fun!" I told them I'd take the program until they could replace me, because these positions were supposed to be given to teachers who wanted to make a little extra money. I didn't want to take their work away.

I had groups ranging from 3rd and 4th-graders to adults, and it was a wonderful learning experience. The kids were great and had tremendous parent support, so there was a minimum amount of problems. My feeling was th any child who behaved himself should be admitted to the after-school program, so naturally the 9th-grade girls attracted boys from some of the others over in the Senior High. One day an older student came up to me during one of the sessions, put his face up against mine and said "How about a dance, babe?" I picked up my hand and really cracked him. Then I was mad at myself for losing myself, which I'd never done before. I asked one of the mothers to watch the class so I could go for a walk. As I was walking down
the hall, the young man came running after me. "Mrs Lishon! Mrs Lishon! PLEASE stop!" I turned around and started to apologize but he cut me off. "Please let me apologize! I was wrong! And I'm a fraternity brother of Chuck's! And I'm a customer of Frank's Drum Shop!"

I was in that program for four years, until shortly after Maurie bought the shop and we decided I couldn't be in two places at the same time."

Chapter Four
Chuck Lishon   1941 - 1978

CHUCK LISHON (RIGHT) WITH FRANK GAULT AND DAD MAURIE

Nurture a bright and inquisitive mind with an environment filled with the top talents in the entertainment business, and the result is bound to be a remarkable talent. From an early age when Chuck burned off excess energy by taking apart the family's stereo and putting it back together, Chuck demonstrated the ability to accomplish anything he set his mind to.

DURING HIS STINT IN THE SERVICE CHUCK WORKED AS A RADIO ANNOUNCER, PRODUCER OF ACTS FOR BASE TALENT SHOWS, AND, OF COURSE, AS A DRUMMER.

THE DRUMMER,

THE SONG-AND-DANCE MAN

Chuck was particularly fascinated with Latin and other ethnic rhythms. The "sound room" at Franks became his domain, and he became one of the top conga players in the Midwest.

(Left) Chuck on a gig with Allen & Rossi at the Edgewater Beach Hotel in 1967.

Maurie-

"Chuck worked at the shop during high school, but it wasn't enough for him- he needed more action. He'd always had a yen for something to do with electronics, and that was when the Moog was starting to come in.

He went to New York and stayed with Beverly and Caroll Bratman (Carroll Musical Instruments) while he worked for the Bratmans. They had three floors of Latin equipment- the largest inventory in the world. Noone had been able to get a handle on taking an inventory, so that's what Chuck went to do.

While he was there, there was one floor that was reserved for rehearsals. They had a synthesizer that was played by a Frenchman named John Jacques. Chuck clung to him like you wouldn't believe to learn as much as he could. When he came back to Chicago, he talked to me and said he wanted to get into the electronics. He contacted Bob Moog and flew to Trumansburg where Moog lived, and laid out the synthesizer the way he wanted it. I don't remember how many months it took to get the instrument, but he got it before he was supposed to, because he went with check in hand. He didn't have the studio ready, so he had to set the synthesizer up in his apratment in Marina City.

He took space where the old Chez Paree used to be; they divided up the building, and the space that he took was exactly where the dance floor and the bandstand and the dressing rooms were when I worked there. The EXACT physical location!

After he'd been there for a while and wanted to expand, he spotted this old Decca building standing empty on LaSalle street. It was nothing but a shell. He formed a combine with some friends, and bought the building. He wasn't in on the building purchase because he didn't have any money, but was very involved in what was going on. He rented a bulldozer, dropped it below the floor, and dug out ten studios.

Chuck sometimes worked around the clock. Finally when it was ready, he put out an album called "The Moog Strikes Bach; Beethoven And Many Others" and it just happened to be a case of bad timing. Walter Carlos had just come out with his big album for Columbia, but they still did very well with it.

They called the studio Sonart and did a lot of jingle recording, and groups, rehearsals.... Buddy Rich rehearsed a band there one day. Chuck recorded it, and Buddy was very happy with it. Buddy said that the next album he did he was going to do with Chuck. There was also a wonderful personal friendship there, but unfortunately Chuck didn't live long enough to record with Buddy."

Chuck died suddenly and unexpectedly in 1978 of a massive heart attack. In a state of near shock, Maurie ordered a full autopsy and was told that Chuck's veins had in places been nearly 3/4 blocked, causing the heart severe stress.

Marty Lishon-

"Losing Chuck changed everything. He was my best friend in the world. His talent was boundless, and he was always two steps ahead of everybody else. He was a lot like the inventor Tesla in that he'd lock in on something until he figured it out- satisfied himself. Then he'd move on to something else. He was the first white guy in the midwest to REALLY get into the Latin thing. He put together the first electronic music studio in Chicago and produced award-winning commercials for companies like United Airlines. On a recent visit to Aleta, we found some of Chuck's notes about polyphonic synthesizers dated 1966-YEARS before such instruments were actually developed. Chuck shot the video that got Cheap Trick started, and music videos were the direction he was headed in when he died. All his studio efforts toward the end were totally geared toward combining music and video, music and film- he was headed where MTV ended up!"

Hans Wurman (left) with Chuck in the studio.

Chapter Five
Maurie buys Franks

I was looking toward the day when I would phase out the drums and have something that would be more of a future than having to go play drums. Just as I was clawing after somebody's heel's when I was a young swinger, there were others now that were clawing after MY heels, waiting for ME to fall.

You've got to get something for security, and business was one of the things that I was interested in. I kept looking in the direction of Frank's Drum Shop. I knew that Frank wanted to sell, and Frank's had always been a haven to me. Jan and I used to meet there even before we were married, when we were both working at the Royale Frolics.

Frank wanted to sell and he couldn't find anybody that could be "Frank", and he couldn't find somebody that had what he had; they didn't have the money. I didn't have the money either, but I could be "Frank". Frank was most enthusiastic, and I was rung in on a deal with two other guys. They wanted to buy the place and they wanted me to front it. I would have had one third and they would have had two-thirds. After we would have got the place paid off, I would have been out in left field with my eyeballs in my ear. Frank was a gentleman about the whole thing. When we went to sign the papers, he said "I want Mr Lishon to be responsible for the other two gentlemen, and I want the other two gentlemen to be responsible for Mr Lishon." This tipped me off to the fact that I shouldn't do it. I walked out on the deal. I made a couple of enemies, but they weren't my friends to begin with, so it didn't make any difference.

When I got home, I got a call from Frank. He said "Maurie, if you're interested in buying my place, you're the kind of a guy I'd like to see Frank's Drum shop go on and on with. Come and see me and we'll talk." I went to see him and we did talk. Anything he wouldn't do for the three of us, he would do for me. He knocked ten thousand dollars off the price. I only had $2,500.00 of my own that I could safely lay my hands on. (I was paying for a house and three kids.) I needed a ten thousand dollar down payment so I borrowed $7,500.00 from one of my brothers. (That $7,500.00 got him over $100,000.00 in fifteen years when I was finally able to buy him out.)

So I bought Frank's Drum Shop in 1959, on August 7th, my birthday. It was retroactive to August the first because the books were on a fiscal year and we stayed that way.

Frank Gault was a very very big influence on my life and I shall never forget him- he was a wonderful man and the fact that I was able to buy the place and carry on with the same traditions and honesty that he had built up all those years is a feather in our cap I would say. The first couple of years that I was there I had to apologize to some of the band directors "to have the audacity to even think of stepping into Frank Gault's shoes".

The funny part of it is that I was a percussionist and Frank was a trombone player originally! But he had built a tremendous reputation for knowledge and service and we really took advantage of it.

"When I bought the place in 1959, it was a hole in the wall on the 5th floor at 226 S Wabash. It's been there for years, but the walls hadn't been cleaned in 22 years. The old place was really filthy dirty, but there was nothing that we could do; there was no way that we could clean it up!"

"Stuff was all over the place. It looked like something that people would talk about all over the world-"You ought to see that old place in Chicago!" We took advantage of the fact that it looked like an 1890's setup. There wasn't a WHOLE lot of inventory, because Frank built a lot of stuff, and repairs were mostly the thing."

"We had a little office in the front, and half the floor. There was a picture frame place that had the back half of the floor. He went out of business about two years after I had taken over the place, so we took over the rest of the floor. (We knocked a little bit of a wall out.)"

VIEW FROM THE BACK (FORMER PICTURE FRAME BUSINESS), SHORTLY AFTER PART OF WALL WAS KNOCKED OUT

"By 1963 you couldn't even walk through the
place because every inch was taken up with something!"

"I'd started to build up a bigger rental business for sounds, for concerts and recordings. It got to the point where we had to do something."

"It still had direct current; when you plugged a vibe in you had to plug it into a converter and it made more noise than the vibe. The bulbs were just hanging, exposed. It would have cost a fortune to bring in new AC lines from the street."

"On the fourth floor the Hertz company had beautiful offices that they vacated, making the place available. I had to make a decision... should I move out of the colorful, dirty, old Frank's and go modern, or should we clean up the dirty old place? Psychologically, I was afraid that I might hurt myself by cleaning up the place. We decided we were going to move down to the fourth floor in 1963."

"People who used to come to see the place were thrilled by the fact that we had made such progress and were now THE Frank's Drum Shop physically that they could see. People used to step off that elevator and look at it with all those drums... We must have had from 50 to 100 sets of drums not counting all the mallet instruments, timpani, chimes..... It was something to see! We were starting to get a lot of publicity- magazines were starting to write us up, etc. We had 4,000 square feet, and the first look when you stepped in off the elevator was startling. In fact one kid stepped off the elevator, took one look, and swallowed his gum.

After I'd been there several years and proven what I could do with the shop (when a lot of people had given me about six months) a lot of them would say to me "Maurie, you've built a reputation and you can stand on your own two feet- why don't you change the name? Why does it have to be Frank's?" My answer was that 'Frank's Drum Shop' is a great name that's known all over the world. We were doing everything we could to keep the reputation and the integrity of the reputation up. One change I DID make was to drop the apostrophe from Frank's, changing it to Franks"

"The only music library that was in there at the start was the Ed Straight system which Frank's owned. I nearly threw it out until I found out that they sold a lot of Ed Straight books. In fact one of the other two men who wanted to purchase Frank's (the deal I walked out on) got in touch with me and said that he thought he should have a finder's fee. As such, all he wanted was the Ed Straight system. I figured if he wanted the Straight System, it must have SOME value so I kept it. We also later published Bobby Christian's snare drum solos with piano accompaniment, and Musser Etudes (4-mallet unaccompanied). From there, Janice started to build up the library. Her name became a byword all over the world with fine percussionists-both performers and especially teachers. We got into practically every college music department and percussion department in the United States, and even out of it. For years people used to come in; traveling symphonies, music educators-making notes and then ordering music. To this day, Janice's name is like magic with percussion music around the world.

A great many of the top performers, especially educators, around the world worked with Jan. She used to get calls all the time asking what was new in percussion music. If something new came into the percussion market, and she heard about it from one of the educators, she would order it. She'd order maybe one copy; if that one went, she'd re-order two. If those two went she would order three, and that's how she built up a library. We used to buy some of the big books 50 and 100 at a time. I remember one inventory that I took one year- the music library alone was around 75,000.00. That's a lot of percussion music. It got so big that Janice had another girl or two that worked in the music library exclusively."

At one point the Lishon's traveled to Germany, and consulted with the reknowned Literature musicologist Dr Carl Schaeffer.

JAN LISHON, STRUGGLING TO MAINTAIN ORDER IN THE MUSIC DEPARTMENT OF THE OVERCROWDED 5TH FLOOR SHOP, SHORTLY BEFORE THE MOVE

"When I started working there, the big drum lines being stocked were Rogers, Slingerland, and Ludwig. Each of those companies made a premium snare drum and a beginner model, and Maurie would display a dozen of each model! That was a whole wall of at least 72 snare drums, and there were more in the back room!" - Mike Balter

Mike Balter:

"I worked at Franks from when I was a young teenager right up until the time I started making Mike Balter mallets. I used to go in for my Saturday morning lesson with uncle Roy, then just hang out after my lesson. It got to the point that when all the regular employees were busy, I'd help out by tuning a drum or changing a head for a customer. I just kept getting more and more involved until I was doing more than some of the paid employees. Finally one Saturday Maurie called me into his office- he said we had a problem to sort out. I couldn't for the life of me figure out what the problem could be- I thought I was helping him out! He asked me what time my lesson was done and I told him 10:00. He said that from then on, if I wasn't out of the shop by 11:00 he was going to pay me for the time I was spending there.

One of the first things I learned working at Frank's was that Maurie hated the color pink. Before he moved down from the fifth floor, he had painted all the walls of the fourth floor pink. Why would someone who hated pink paint all the walls of his new shop that color? It was because he wanted to be sure that every square inch was covered with display merchandise. Maurie worked hard at making sure that the first impression visitors got when they came off the elevator was overwhelming.... It was a drummer's fantasyland! I don't want to get corny here, but it reminds me of 'The Wizard Of Oz' where the movie is in black and white until you get to OZ, then everything is in color. It was like that for any percussionist who visited Frank's! Everywhere you looked was merchandise, and the first time visitor was stunned. If Maurie saw pink at the top of a stack of drum heads, it meant that I wasn't keeping the stock up fast enough, and he let me know about it."

"There were stacks and stacks of drum outfits. None of them had the tom-tom holders mounted. All the drum outfits that came in were shipped from the manufacturer with the tom holder in a bag. This was because we installed so many Roger's mounts on Ludwig outfits, etc. The customer picked out the brand and color of outfit he wanted, then decided on the hardware and the drums went back for Clarence (or sometimes myself) to drill and install the hardware.

Maurie never wanted a customer to buy something he didn't really need- even if he wanted it! I once saw a father (from a wealthy Chicago suburb) come in to buy his son a Ludwig 'Blue Note' outfit. (This was the largest cataloged Ludwig outfit, with two bass drums.) After chatting with the guy a little, Maurie wouldn't sell it to him. He got out a practice pad, stand, and pair of sticks and laid them out on the counter. He told him to buy these items and come back in a few weeks to talk about the big drum set."

On the other hand, there were many many times when a student really needed an instrument, but couldn't afford it. Again, Maurie looked out for their best interests. This was before the days of credit cards, so the only methods of payment were cash, check, or putting it on the 'house account'. Carrying on the tradition established by Frank Gault, Maurie helped out the students and working drummers by letting them take the equipment they needed, and working out mutually acceptable payment plans for each one. This meant he had to be a good judge of character, because he carried from $50,000.00 to $75,000.00 a month on 'house accounts'!"

Dr. Ben F Miller (Marshall University) has more to say about Maurie's personal involvement with his customers-

"Even though I have studied with some outstanding teachers, it was Maurie who really taught me how to practice. I was working on my senior recital and Maurie asked me how it was going. I said there were places that I kept making the same mistake over and over. I just couldn't get it worked out. Maurie said that I should practice the measure with the mistake repeatedly and slowly. Then play the measure in front of the mistake measure and hook the two together, then practice the measure after the mistake measure repeatedly, then hook those two measures together. Finally hook the three measures together and play them slowly at first and then faster and faster. I have been practicing that same way ever since and I have my students do the same thing.

Maurie personally drove out to our house 25 miles from the shop to set up my first drum set while I was at school so that my parents could surprise me when I got home.

As a college percussion student I went to the shop to purchase some Saul Goodman snare drum sticks. The sticks were kept in a bin. Unmatched. I started rolling them across the counter and some of them were really badly warped. As the indignant student, I pointed it out to Maurie and he agreed that some of the sticks were in pretty poor shape. So right then and there he called Goodman in New York and started kidding him. "I've got Benny Miller here, and George Gaber told him to buy some of your sticks and we can't find any two that are matched! How can I send him back to Indiana University and have him say that he purchased these sticks at Franks Drum Shop?" He went on and on. I was really flabbergasted. I ended up buying a pair of Premier sticks which I still have.

Early in my professional career things were not going very well and I came to Chicago for a visit and of course I went down to the shop. I started crying the blues to Maurie who would have none of it. He basically told me to straighten up and fly right and quit feeling sorry for myself. He was right, of course. Right at that moment I needed a kick in the butt more than I needed a sympathetic shoulder to cry on.

One day in the mid 60's a man in his 20's came into the store and was talking to Maurie. He was complaining that the leader he was working for only hired him for weddings and bar mitzvahs, but when there was a big gig like an industrial show or something like that, the leader would hire someone else. Maurie put down his cigar, leaned over the counter to the guy and really lit into him. He said "When I was your age I was happy to get any gig I could. I had three drum sets. One at the theater, one at home and one in my car. I was just happy to get a call for any gig I could get. You're making money, quit complaining. If you practiced more you might get good enough to play the bigger shows." The guy just nodded.

In the early 70's I was at the shop when Jim Ganduglia, the drummer for Johnny Mathis, called from California. He had an Acme siren that was making a rattling sound. Maurie went and got one from the drawer and went through all the steps for taking it apart, where to put some pencil graphite, how to adjust the spindle, and how to put it back together. He had Jim blow it into the phone for all of us to hear.

I was in the store one day just before Christmas. A businessman came into the shop and said to Maurie that he wanted to purchase a drum set for his teenage son. This was around the time of the Beatles. The man pointed to a red sparkle set in the corner and said he wanted that one. Maurie asked the man if his son played in the school band. The man said no. Maurie asked if the son played drums. The man said no. After it was all said and done, Maurie gave the man the name of a teacher near his home and sold him a pair of sticks, a practice pad, and a Haskell Harr method book. He told him that once his son learned to play they could come back and purchase a drum set. I just can't imagine that ever happening at a retail store in this day and age.

A family came into the shop to purchase a high hat for their son. They didn't have a lot of money and could not afford a pair of Zildjian hihats. (This must have been about 1963 or '64.) Maurie picked out a good Zildjian 14" cymbal for the top and a lesser quality cymbal for the bottom. He told the parents that when they could afford a better cymbal to come back and he would match up a Zildjian for the bottom and they could trade the other in or use it as a crash cymbal.

In 1978 I brought a bunch of my percussion students from Marshall University in West Virginia up to Chicago on a field trip and Al Payson gave a snare drum clinic for them at the back of the shop.

I was visiting with Larry Linkin, the president of Slingerland, at the Slingerland factory when he got the call that Chuck Lishon had died. My mother accompanied me to the funeral. It seemed as though all of musical Chicago was there. It was as if one of our own family had died."

OPENING DAY POSE DUPLICATION

On the 30th Anniversary of the opening of Franks Drum Shop, Maurie "recreated" the original opening day photo (see page 8) with as many of the original individuals as possible, in the same positions.

From the left: Dick Craft (son-in-law of Amrawco founder Howard Emrie), Roy Knapp (in place of Ralph Smith), Frank Gault, John Noonan, Bob Jamison (manager of Franks at the time, in place of Ed Shebanek), Bobby Christian, Maurie Lishon, Josephine Christian, and Chuck Lishon (in place of Ormond Downes).

SUZANNE LISHON

"I started out with Franks Drum Shop like so many young employees... pushing a broom. All part of the "gig". I was the Lishon with the low profile and followed in my mother's footsteps of being a dancer. I helped in the office, filing, answering phones, typing statements, and making up the library file system. You know the clerical stuff everybody still hates to do! In those days it was women's work- yuk!

Though I never worked in sales, I did the things that were fun and didn't tie me down to hours and staying on the premises. Clarence Williams taught me how to tuck a calf head which quickly became passe. I knew how to pick out a good set of drum sticks and always tested them first... Dad used to say "The sticks are straight, the glass is bumpy!" I often made the signs that were posted all around the shop and helped with inventories, especially in sheet music and drum method books.

Actually, the best part of my deal was as long as I was willing to make the factory pick ups, I could have a car- which was very cool in 1963 for a teenage girl to have a car full time. So there I was, me and my girlfriend, Sondra, making trips to Slingerland, to see Hal Trommer at Deagan, Knappe Music House and miscellanous suppliers whose names at the present escape me, to pick up stock. The guys on the docks loved us. Boy, I could zip my car into a loading dock in no time. I'd pretend it was a semi, of course, and out to impress. I made it my business to do small deliveries to rock concerts as much as possible and then stay for the concert- an FDS perk, of course.

I also hung out during clinics whenever I could, even after I was married, had children, and got divorced. I was an extra pair of eyes to watch the crowd. We certainly did have crowds. Franks Drum Shop drew incredible amounts of people, all ages, sizes, shapes, and colors. It was wonderful, free... electric."

"I continued the family tradition of musicians with my children. Michael (born in 1970) and B.J. (born in 1975) studied drums with Phil Stanger starting in 1978. Today Michael is one of L.A.'s up and coming jazz drummers (He's also one hell of a blues guitar player). B.J. plays keyboards, saxophone, guitar, and some drums but is making a living as an actor. Two incredibly talented children!

Me, I'm a Producer and writing children's books that I'm sure will take off and capture the hearts of children both young and old... just as soon as I find a publisher!

I am very grateful for the legacy of talent, from both my parents, that I have been so priviledged to carry on."

(left) Michael got an early start in the family tradition!
(below) B.J.(left) and Michael Dubin-Lishon

**MAURIE (3rd from right) WITH WM F LUDWIG JR ON HIS LEFT AND
LUDWIG SALES MANAGER FRANK PEPPLER ON HIS RIGHT**

Visits from representatives of the Ludwig company (as well as the other major companies) were frequent as they lobbied for orders and checked out the competition. Looking over the new 1967 Ludwig catalog are (L to R): Bobby Christian, Roy Knapp, Peppler, Maurie, Ludwig, and Chuck Lishon.

Such visits often resulted not just in a large order for the manufacturer, but often an agreement of a unique nature. Franks, for example, usually purchased the entire NAMM music convention exhibits from most of the major manufacturers including Ludwig. Sometimes arrangements were made for limited-edition instruments such as the brass-shell suprasphonic 400 snare drum which Ludwig made without a snare bed exclusively for Maurie and Bob Yeager of the Pro Drum Shop.

MAURIE-
"There was a great deal of research done on our floor with some of the men from the different manufacturers. Hundreds of people (including Japs with cameras) did a lot of research on our premises. We guinea-pigged a lot of ideas for them and I came up with a few ideas here and there.

I did some research for the Ludwig Drum Company because in those days they used to use hot lights for television. You could die in a rehearsal in the studios it got so hot. Jewelry and certain drum finishes, or brass instruments when turned in a certain direction would produce those black, brilliant 'globs' that would really spoil the scene. In doing research, we came up with the finish that was called black diamond on the drums, and we used to have to soap some of the metal stands, hardware, things like that that were on the stage (especially with the drum hardware) so that those globs didn't come up. Finally we determined that if we satinized all the chrome and glossy metal finishes it minimized the 'globbing'.

We started making our own concert tambourines, a concert slapstick, the segue stick, mark chimes, and the rock-a-rine (hi-hat tambourine attachment)... We were the first ones to bring in Valje and Gon-Bop congas east of the Rocky Mountains. Al Payson and I designed what we called the PAM-case (Percussion, Accessories, and Mallets).

MAURIE'S PLAYING DAYS CONTINUE....

CBS WBBM
c. 1960

When Maurie purchased Frank's Drum Shop, he did not immediately give up on his playing career. He continued to answer calls for all sorts of gigs, and kept his position on staff at CBS.

Maurie-
"I was at WBBM a total of almost 20 years. Whe I was first hired, Caesar told me this job was for eight weeks and if you didn't get your notice on a Friday, you had eight more weeks at least. I lived by that through all those years. After I'd been there for fourteen years, suddenly I received my eight weeks notice. At the same time there were three other fellas that got their eight-week notice. At this point in time there were no live shows coming out of WBBM at all. We were just picking up a check on Friday because the economy department was out to prove that they didn't need any more live music and so for two years they had planned not to have a live note coming out of there to prove their point. We weren't playing, just getting paid. By this time I had already purchased Frank's Drum Shop so I figured 'what the hell...'

It seems somebody got the brainstorm (with the civil rights movement afoot) to bring three blacks on the staff. As a result of that four of us had gotten our notice and they were bringing in a bass player by the name of "Truck" Parnum, a saxophone player by the name of Frank Derrick, a trumpet played by the name of Art Hoyle, and the fourth man, it turned out, was Bob Tilles, who had left the station a couple of years before. (How he got involved in this thing I'll never know, but it sounds funny, doesn't it?) Anyway, three of us who had gotten our notice were first-chair men, and the fourth, a bass player by the name of Bob Fassbender who had only been on the staff about six months.

I took my eight weeks notice gracefully because it was only an eight-weeks job when I had started fourteen years before that. I just took it for granted that was it, forgot all about it, and at the end of eight weeks I was through. That gave me more time to dedicate full time to the shop which I was doing practically anyway because we had no live shows.

Six or eight weeks later, I got a call. (The Chicago Federation of Musicians was in trusteeship at the time. Hal Davis who later became the national president was the official trustee.) I got a call from some of the guys that there was going to be a big mass meeting at the union, of all of the radio staff players and they wanted me to be there. I'd been through at the station already and I told them "What am I gonna do there?" They said "We just want you to come." Porky and Joe Rumoro were especially rough on my showing up. They said if I don't show up, they're going to come and get me and I knew they weren't kidding.

The day of the meeting I jumped in a cab and went over from the shop to the meeting. The union floor was loaded- all the staffs and guys who had been in radio were there, so you're talking close to 200 men. I'm sitting between Porky and Joe Romero and they're both poking me to get up and say something. I said "What do you want me to say?" They said "Just get up something cause whatever you say will be the right thing anyway." I finally stood up and introduced myself. I told Hal Davis that I was Maurie Lishon and I'd been the staff drummer at WBBM for 14 years. As I looked around and saw all these men that I'd worked with in night clubs and "upholstered sewers" and theaters and radio stations who had paid their dues for many years, I said I felt it was a little tough to expect them all to be thrown out into the open market for a jobbing date on a Saturday night, to compete with fellas that had that stuff locked up.

At this stage of their lives to have to go in to make a living, I felt pretty badly because at least I had worked something out and I owned my own business. I felt a little more stable and I thought is was a dirty shame for them to be treated that way. That was the extent of it, and I went back to my business. Several weeks later (not too long before Christmas; we were probably fourteen or fifteen deep at the shop) I got a call. I'd forgotten all about the WBBM incident. The voice identifies himself as Hal Davis. At first I thought it was a gag. He asked if I was the same Maurie Lishon at BBM, I said yes, he said "We've been meeting, how would you like to go back on your staff job?" "I'd LOVE it." "You'll be hearing from us."

About four weeks later I got a call from Frank Smith. (Caesar Petrillo had passed away and Frank Smith was the musical director.) He asked how I'd like to come back on staff. "I'd Love it!" "Okay, you start back on Jan. 8th and the time you've been off will be figured as leave of absence; you're still first-chair man."

I went back on staff for another couple of years. There was not much to play, so I very seldom even had to report. Pennies from heaven, but now that I look back at some of the things, I really earned it.

After we all went back on staff except for Bob Fassbender he turned around and sued the station in a civil court for prejudice in reverse. He won his case and they had to take him back on staff and pay him retroactively for the time he was off and they couldn't fire him for the duration of the contract."

The Eastman School of Music Marimba Ensemble, on the Ed Sullivan Show.
(from left) Vivian Emery, Jane Burnett, Edward DeMatteo, Gordon Peters, Ronald Barnett, Sullivan, and Mitchell Peters. (not pictured: Peter Tanner)

There was a variety program on the CBS network for many years called 'The Ed Sullivan Show' or they called it 'Toast of The Town'. One year they decided that they were going to do the show from different parts of the country.

The way we did it in Chicago, the video crew went around different parts of Chicago and shot different scenes, and then we did the audio track at the studio. We had a big production number; they had a big line of dancing girls, and stars.... We did one big production number that featured Dolores Grey who was a pretty hot property at that time- a very talented woman. We had this production arrangement with a vocal on 'Alexander's Ragtime Band'. We were using about a thirty-piece orchestra and the conductor was Ray Block who had the show for years. There were about six or seven pages of manuscript, and we got down to one section where there was a tempo change... actually it was not a tempo change; we were in 2 and we went into 4 but the tempo was the same. We call that listesso. There were eight bars of sound effects cues on the drum part at that point and I'd never had any problem cueing acts-you know; I was 'Mr Drummer- catch everything!' that was my meat. So what we did, we get to this part and I can see that what the choreographer (who's working out in front of the band) was doing didn't coincide with what was written in my parts. So I stopped the band and asked them to take it back a couple of bars before the change. They did, but I could see that we were still confronted with the same problem. I said "Let's take it again, a little bit slower, from the same place." It turned out that it was written one quarter note off, which made the whole thing look like a comedy act instead of catching what was going on onstage. We got it straightened out, but then after we did, half the guys in the band came to me and said "Why didn't you leave it alone? We could've gotten more overtime if you'd have waited and stretched it out a little."

"Carol Channing played the Empire Room at the Palmer House with her one-woman act. She had her own group, but she wasn't happy with her drummer- (getting all the cues). They came over to me and asked if I could help them out by building the cues the way that they would like them; I said sure, and arranged a whole new set of cue sheets. As a result of that, they asked us to stay for dinner in the Empire Room. We're sitting there, and who walks over but Freddie Townsend, the PR man for the Empire Room- he was an old friend of ours from the Royale Frolics. The cake was for the 200th anniversary of the show she was doing."

Maurie:
"When any symphony in the world was on tour anywhere near Chicago, the percussionists would get to Frank's by hook or crook and spend hours or days at the shop, browsing, buying, and doing research."

(Above) Morris Lang (L), and Saul Goodman (C), principal percussionist and tympanist with the New York Philharmonic, with Maurie (1973)
(Below) Al Payson (L) of the Chicago Symphony, Maurie, and Ron Fink, head of the percussion department at North Texas State University

Jan: "Al and Ron went to the University of Illinois in Champaign together. Fellow drummers and students always used to use Franks as a meeting place. That's where the phrase "home away from home" originated.

(above) In 1967 Maurie and Jan were invited to visit Ed Shaughnessy; he was doing the Johnny Carson show, which at that time was still being taped in the NBC studios in New York.
(below) (from left) Maurie, Frank Gault, Bobby Christian, John Noonan, Roy Knapp, and Dick Craft

Chapter Six - Equipment

For much of his career, Maurie played on "skin" drum heads. This was an added challenge to drummers who were were gigging before the days of plastic heads, especially when one into situations such as this one, when he was with Ramona's band...

"We had a couple weeks booked at the Roosevelt Hotel in New Orleans. The big room there was always called the Blue Room but they would change the name of it depending on the motif and the decor of the room. Well, when we played there it was called the Hawaiian Blue Room and inside they had big palm trees growing and everything... On the bandstand behind the back row where the drums and brass would be, there was a sheet-metal setup with water that used to drop from the ceiling. Before every show they would put on a pseudo-rainstorm and have lightning flashes in the room- it was very effective. The only trouble was that in those days they didn't have plastic heads, all we had was calf heads. By the time that rainstorm that was so beautiful was finished and we had to go in and do a show, my heads were like pieces of tissue paper from the dampness. It wasn't easy, but you learn to adapt."

Phil Stanger did the field test for the first plastic heads that were shipped to Frank's Drum Shop (still owned by Frank Gault at the time) for evaluation. He was working for Barnes and Carruthers outdoor carnivals, doing 4 days in Hurley, Wisconsin. The heads, made by Evans, had two wooden flesh hoops which were held together by rivets. Stanger took a Ludwig mahogany 6 1/2" drum with the prototype Evans heads for the weekend. He was playing a number with brushes on the fourth day when the head exploded! Shattered like a pane of glass. The plastic head had been sand-blasted to roughen the surface so the brushes would have friction. This sandblasting weakend the head and the grain let go. Ludwig's first heads did the same at the hands of Buddy Rich.

Maurie is shown here at the first plastic drum head demonstration to take place at a NAMM show, in July of 1957 at Chicago's Palmer House Hotel.

The issue of exactly whom invented the most secure hoop mounting of a plastic drum head is a complicated one. So many people started to work with mylar as a drum head material at about the same time that it became more a question of who PERFECTED the best head mounting first. And that question became a bitterly disputed legal issue with Evans taking Remo to court, and Ludwig taking legal action against Slingerland. While Wm. F. Ludwig Sr. first claimed to have no knowledge of the head mounting technology used in the Camco drum head until 1959, Bud Slingerland was able to dispute this by producing a receipt proving Ludwig had purchased a Camco drum head from Franks Drum Shop in November of 1957. Mr. Ludwig was then 85 years of age at the time of the trial in 1965. Mr. Ludwig's mounting invention prevailed in the marketplace over time. "I would rather have not gotten involved," says Maurie. "But Bud knew we had a copy of the receipt and said I could volunteer it to him or he could subpeona it...."

B. The Claims in Issue are Also Invalid
    Because of the Camco Drumhead

In his second deposition Mr. Slingerland disclosed that he had a copy of an invoice from Frank's Drum Shop in Chicago, Illinois, showing the sale in 1957 of a Camco drumhead to Ludwig Drum Co.

Excerpt from a Post-Trial Brief, Civil Action #3965, United States District Court For The Middle District of Tennessee, Nashville Division.

THE FIRST "PRESENTATION" WAS A HEAD MADE BY CEMENTING TWO PIECES OF IRISH LINEN TOGETHER FOR THE BATTER HEAD AND USING ONE PIECE FOR THE SNARE HEAD. THEY WERE FOLDED OVER AND GLUED TO THE WOOD FLESH HOOP. THESE PROVED VERY UNSATISFACTORY FOR SNARE DRUMS BUT THEY WERE USED TO A LIMITED EXTENT ON BASS DRUMS WHERE TONE AND DURABILITY WERE NOT IMPORTANT. A FEW YEARS LATER AN IMPROVED FORMULA OF LACQUER APPEARED ON THE MARKET AND A FEW DRUM MANUFACTURERS SPRAYED IT ON BOTH SIDES OF HEADS FOR A COATING THAT WAS SUPPOSED "TO KEEP OUT THE DAMPNESS." AFTER A FEW PLAYING SESSIONS THE LACQUER WORE OFF AND THE CALF HEADS REVERTED TO THEIR OLD TRICKS. THEN CAME THE FIRST SHEET PLASTIC IDEA. AT THAT TIME PLASTIC SHEETING HAD NOT REACHED THE STAGE OF PERFECTION THAT IT HAS TODAY. IT WAS, HOWEVER, HAILED AS A GREAT ACHIEVEMENT AND ADVERTISED WIDELY, BUT IT SOON FELL BY THE WAYSIDE BECAUSE IT WAS VERY HARD TO PLAY ON AND BROKE EASILY. SEVERAL YEARS HAVE PASSED BETWEEN THEN AND THE PRESENT DAY TYPE OF PLASTIC SHEETING WHICH IS MADE BY THE DU PONT COMPANY AND CALLED "MYLAR"®. M. L. EVANS, THEN RESIDING IN SANTA FE, NEW MEXICO, WAS THE FIRST TO DISCOVER IT AS BEING IDEAL FOR DRUM HEADS.

Cuts from early promotional materials from Evans Products, Inc.

MAURIE WITH ONE OF THE FIRST ROGERS DYNA-SONIC SNARE DRUMS

When the first Dyna-Sonic came to Frank's, Phil Stanger purchased it, but was asked to leave it on display at Frank's so it could be seen until production geared up and more units started to come in.

Maurie:
"Henry Grossman bought Rogers as a tax write-off. He hadn't really planned on it becoming such a successful drum line. What happened was Joe Thompson- he redesigned the line and was the main reason the Rogers line became so successful."

Though the name was Frank's DRUM Shop, cymbals were obviously a very important part of the business. Until quite recently every cymbal was completely different and unique. (This is still true with most brands, though a few pride themselves on uniformity of tone.) For this reason it was much easier for drummers to buy cymbals from a shop such as Frank's, where there was a huge selection. Maurie found this out early in his career...

"This happened when Frank's Drum Shop was still the Dixie Music House. About two days before we closed at the Palace and were about to leave town, I went up to Frank Gault and told him I'd like to listen to some cymbals. He said 'Help yourself!' I went through a whole raft of cymbals. I don't know how it is with other drummers, but with me, I know when 'the lights go on', you're hearing something! And I hit this one cymbal and the lights really went on. So I said I'd love to buy it, but I owed him about 20.00 already. He never sent out any bills and never put the pressure on, but I didn't want to get in too deep. He says "Take it over to the theater and try it." I said okay, if it's ok with you. So I took it over to the theater and I loved it-it was a wonderful cymbal for catching kicks. So... comes Thursday afternoon, we're closing Thursday night and leaving town first thing in the morning. Much as I wanted that cymbal, I didn't want to put any more money on the books with Frank so I brought it back and said "Frank, I love this cymbal, but I can't afford to buy it now." He said "Just put your name on the inside of the bell, and maybe when you come back if it's still here you won't have to hit all the cymbals." Which I did. When I could afford it I went back and found that same cymbal. I still use it today, and it's one of the best cymbals I ever played."

FRANK GAULT LATHING A CYMBAL ON A VISIT TO THE ZILDJIAN FACTORY

There were many things about Frank's that Maurie did not change, including the manner in which cymbals were displayed. For years Maurie continued to stack the cyymbals on edge behind the counter. All of the Zildjian cymbals were received with no markings whatsoever except the trademark stamp. Zildjian agreed to ship the cymbals this way to Frank's because of the tremendous depth of inventory they carried and because of their skill in selecting and grading cymbals.

Cymbal selection is an art... Maurie had a complete set of rubber stamps. If a customer called and said they had to have a 20" medium-thin-crash, someone would carefully go through the 20" cymbals until they found "the" cymbal. It would be stamped appropriately, and shipped out.

Jan Lishon dancing with Len DiMuzio at the party thrown by Zildjian when they opened the new A. Zildjian plant in Norwell, MA, c. 1970.

Len was not only "sales manager", but one of the ace cymbal selectors for Zildjian. If Buddy or Louie needed a certain sound, they'd call Lennie and describe what they were looking for. For a time during the 70's, Zildjian even marketed the selection service. The customer could specify that he wanted, say, a pair of 13" hi-hats with a matching 15" crash and 18" ride. After a timbre-matched set was selected from the Zildjian vaults, each cymbal of the set would be stamped 'Special Selection'.

(Cymbal selection is a service that Zildjian still provides to this day, though they are no longer stamped 'Special Selection'.)

Lennie is currently Director of Artist Relations & Education. He has been with Zildjian for 32 years.

Maurie and Jan Lishon with Robert Paiste at the Paiste plant in Nottvil, Switzerland, 1967.

Arthur Fiedler was delighted when he discovered this instrument tucked away in the 'sound room' at Frank's. He'd thought Turkey was the only place to find one of these.

Also referred to as The Turkish Crescent or 'jingling Johnny', this instrument is considered absolutely essential for late eighteenth and early nineteenth-century marches.

Note the gongs on the wall behind Maurie. Frank's stocked gongs not only from the cymbal companies, but also imported some directly from China.

MAURIE HOLDING A SCHELLENBAUM

Marty Lishon, trying out a set of gamelons

Jan and Maurie in 1991, holding a cymbal presented to them by the Zildjian family in 1976. The cymbal (since donated to the Percussive Arts Society Museum) is autographed by Avedis Zildjian and his sons Armand Zildjian and Robert Zildjian.

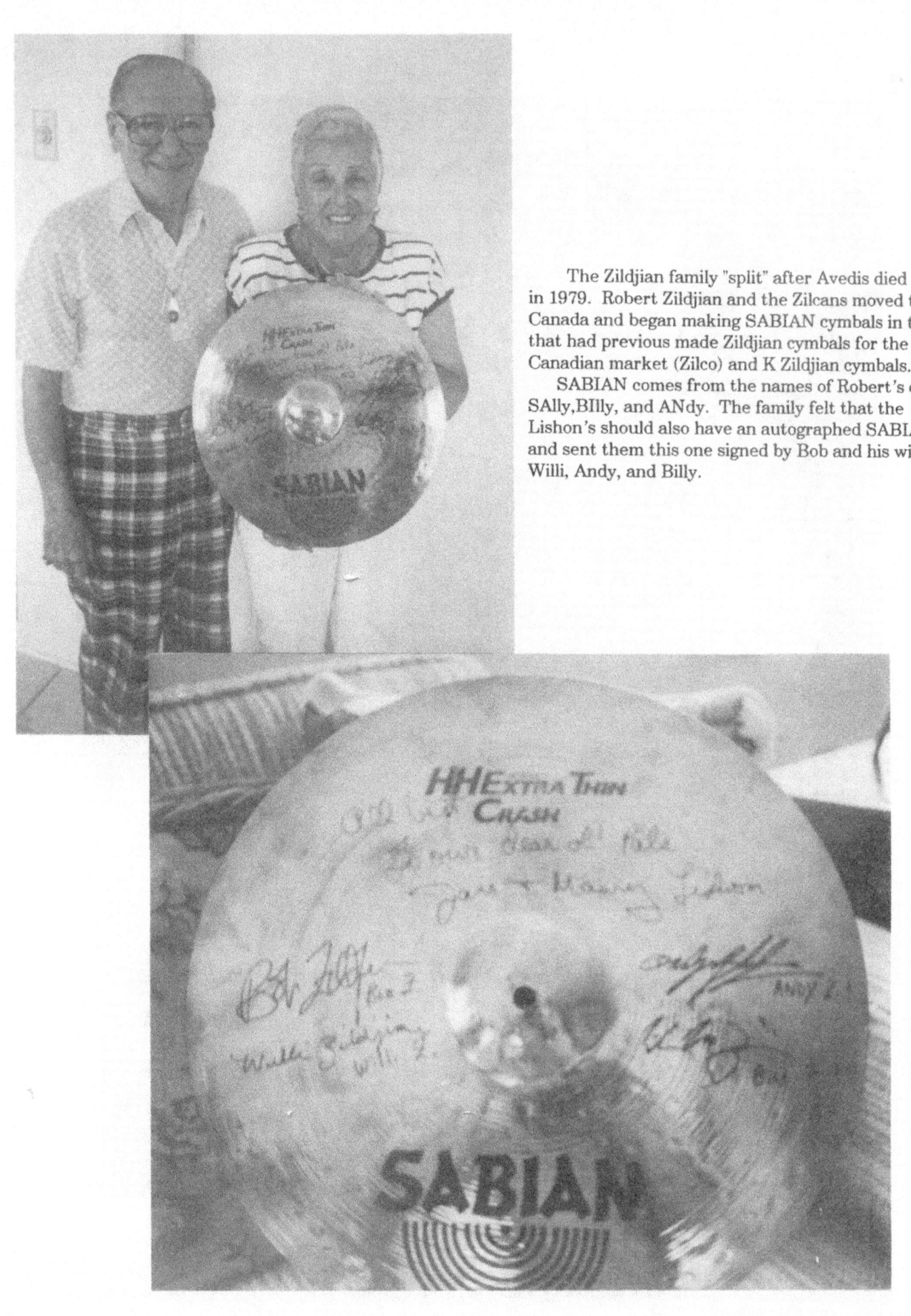

The Zildjian family "split" after Avedis died in 1979. Robert Zildjian and the Zilcans moved to Canada and began making SABIAN cymbals in the plant that had previous made Zildjian cymbals for the Canadian market (Zilco) and K Zildjian cymbals.

SABIAN comes from the names of Robert's children; SAlly, BIlly, and ANdy. The family felt that the Lishon's should also have an autographed SABIAN, and sent them this one signed by Bob and his wife Willi, Andy, and Billy.

JOE MORELLO (above) demonstrating a Fibes outfit, playing MF "mit feeling" (below) with Suzanne Lishon, Gene Krupa and two customers of Franks

HINGER TIMPANI INTRODUCTION

Front row, from left: Billy Hyde, Gary Kristao, Ed Poremba, Bob Zildjian, Gordon Peters
Back row, from left: Bobby Christian, Roy Knapp, Al Payson, Bill Schinstine, Sandy Feldstein, Jackie Meyer, Bev Bratman, Dave Ordell, Jan Lishon, Maurie Lishon, Leo White, Fred Hinger, Tom Akins, Sam Denov, Tele Lesbine, Neal Fluegel, Bill Ludwig Jr., and Don Canedy

86

BARRETT DEEMS

Maurie:

"You can't talk about Barrett Deems with just a few words. He's a great drummer, even today! I'm 79 and Barrett is older than I am and playing his CAN off! And he's still as big a character as he ever was.

Barrett used to traipse in and out of the shop-always with an entourage... He always seemed to have four or five kids following him. On this particular day (when my office was in the middle of the shop), I had broken my thumb and had it all bandaged up. Barrett was in with his little group and we were fooling around a little.

We used to sell a stick called the Vito stick. This was a Franks Drum Shop product that was invented by tympanist Ben Vito. It was a combination stick; one side was soft, for tympani, and the other side was a rosewood ball for bells and snare drum and things like that where you needed a hard surface very quickly until you could change mallets. That stick was very important to us.

Barrett was up in the front of the shop, but the Wabash Avenue windows, with these kids looking at some stuff. Somebody says to me "Why don't you put him on?" So I said Ok, I would. I put a snare drum in the office and had somebody say to Barrett "Maurie says he can play more with one hand than you can with two!" Barrett says "Yeah. Sure."

I took my left hand (with the broken thumb) and stuck it out of the doorway of my office so he could see it from the front of the shop. I took this mallet.... If you know what to do with it, if you describe a figure eight and you've got a head with any friction on it, you can play a one-handed roll and continue and continue. I said "Listen!" Barrett says "We're listening!" I started this thing and it goes rrrrrRRRRRRrrrrrrRRRRRRRrrrrrrr. It continued on and on while I'm holding my hand out where he can see it. He knows I'm doing it with one hand, and in his own inimitable way he yells "MAURIE! IT'S A TRICK!!" "

Checking out Maurie's broken thumb- (from left): **Jim Ross, Roy Knapp, Joe Cusatis, Lou Singer, Haskell Harr, Bob Rosengarden, Maurie, and Frank Gault**

Chapter Seven
The Mystique of Franks

It wasn't so much the sheer quantity of drum equipment, the music, the presence of countless drum personalities, or the remarkable customer service that really built the mystique at Frank's. The things that rounded out the picture were the repair shop, the 'sound room', the teaching staff, and the clinics. All together, these factors made for an unbeatable combination.

CLARENCE WILLIAMS AT THE WORKBENCH

Rather extraordinary feats are expected of a repair technician at a world-class drum shop. Clarence was sometimes referred to as 'the doctor of the operation' because he could rebuild and repair almost any type of percussion instrument and construct different sound devices.

Clarence once had to modify a set for use by a midget who led his own band. A floor tom was converted to a bass drum, and all the stands were cut down accordingly.

THE BACK ROOM AT FRANKS, c. 1963

In this shot of the back room at Franks, you can see a few of the percussion oddities from around the world. Rentals to performing musicians and studios became a significant part of Franks business. The Harmonicats always made Franks one of their first stops, where they rented castanet machines, finger cymbals, a variety of tambourines, and a few drums.

Ramsey Lewis' drummer once rented a Chinese funeral gong, an assortment of cowbells, and a surf box. Trini Lopez rented a 30" timpany for "Zorba The Greek".

One of the top producers of broadcast commercials who was a good customer of Frank's was Bill Walker, of Bill Walker Productions. He frequently would phone before he even wrote the commercials, to check on what unique sounds were available. On one visit he dug through the bell collection to find eight specialized sounds, including a B- scale and some graduated Mayan bells. He then scored the commercials himself and was ready to record as soon as he got to the studio.

One day an ad agency wanted to duplicate the sound of someone tapping on a washing machine. Clarence put together a contraption made primarily from a set of steel shelving, which Chuck dubbed the 'Norge rap-tap simulator'.

Another situation that called for creativity was when the Chicago Symphony Orchestra presented "Sinfonia India" and needed a string of deer hoofs, a yaqui metal rattle, and a water gourd. The yaqui metal rattle ended up being a toilet float with shot in it.

The effects collection included wind and rain machines, lion roars, cuckoo mating calls, a string of butterfly cocoons, and other hard-to-find sound effects. (Some of these were relics from Frank Gault's days of selling effects to theater drummers.)

RED NORVO and his orchestra, at the Commodore Hotel in New York, 1938

Red Norvo was a longtime friend and customer of Maurie, and of Frank Gault before him.
Maurie:

"There was a little boy about 10 or 11 years old who came into Franks Drum Shop with his father one day. He wanted to know if we handled Red Norvo's slap mallets. I said "Certainly". He asked "Well... can I see a pair?" I said "Certainly." I gave him the pair, and he said "Can I try them?" I said "Certainly." So he went over to a vibe and he started to fool around with it. He wasn't much of a player, but he had something in mind and the fact that he was interested in Red Norvo mallets was interesting to us. Red happened to be in the back talking to my repair man about some bongos or something, so I went in back and I got Red. I said "There's a kid out there who's interested in your mallets. Let's go out there and see what happens." Red went out, and got behind the little boy. From behind him, he took the mallets out of his hand and started to play around. The kid wondered what was happening, so he turned around and looked up and saw Red Norvo and he screamed. Absolutely SCREAMED! I bet to this day if you could find that kid and ask him about the day he met Red Norvo, you'd really get an earful!

But that's the kind of guy Red was, God Bless him. He was just elected to the PAS hall of fame last year (1992), and I can't think of anybody more deserving."

PRESENTS

Swinging Super Seminar Series of '68
FREE Percussion Clinics

> The most impressive clinic lineup ever was announced for 1968; this is a reduced version of the poster-flyer promotional piece.

STARTING with ROY BURNS (Courtesy Rogers Drum Co.)

FEBRUARY 24, 1968

to celebrate the 30th Anniversary of our opening at 226 South Wabash Avenue as Chicago's _first_ exclusive Drum Shop

WATCH FOR THE DATES OF THIS STAR STUDDED LINEUP OF PLAYERS—ALL CLINICS STARTS AT 2 P.M. AT

- BOBBY CHRISTIAN (Courtesy Ludwig Drum Co.)
- GENE KRUPA (Courtesy Slingerland Drum Co.)
- JOE MORELLO (Courtesy Ludwig Drum Co.)
- BOBBY ROSENGARDEN (Courtesy Premier Drum Co.)
- JOE CUSATIS (Courtesy Slingerland Drum Co.)
- JERRY COLEMAN (Courtesy of Premier Drum Co.)
- LOUIS BELLSON (Courtesy of Roger Drum Co.)
- JAKE JERGER'S "54 HEADS" (Courtesy Slingerland Drum Co.)
- PAUL GUERRERO (Courtesy Sonor Drum Co.)
- ED SHAUGHNESSY (Courtesy of Rogers Drum Co.)

AND OTHERS

Maurie Lishon cordially invites you to be his guest at America's oldest and largest exclusive percussion center

percussion center of america
FRANKS DRUM SHOP, inc.

ENTIRE 4th FLOOR
226 SOUTH WABASH AVENUE
CHICAGO, ILLINOIS

TELEPHONE
WAbash 2-1300
HArrison 7-8440

(Above) Lionel Hampton giving Maurie some tips on handling multiple mallets.
(Below) Hamp was appearing at The London House with Roy Burns filling the drum seat. Maurie had made arrangements for Roy to do a clinic at Franks, and Hamp joined him.

Bobby Christian

Franks was a second home to Bobby Christian, from his Paul Whiteman days (above) through the 1970's when he maintained a teaching studio on the premises. Bobby was inducted into the Percussive Arts Society Hall of Fame in 1989, the same year as Maurie Lishon. (He passed away in 1991.) His introduction at the PAS banquet follows here, his acceptance speech is on page 132.

"Our first honoree this evening has had an illustrious career. He is the musician's musician who has earned a world-wide reputation as a composer, arranger, conductor, and as the dean of total percussion. Bobby's prestigious career includes the Paul Whiteman Orchestra, NBC, and ABC network orchestras. Over 40 years as one of America's top studio percussionists for recordings, films, commercials, television. Every person I have talked with about Bobby uses the same adjective- energy! I saw it again at the jam session last night as he went from vibes to drum set; enthusiastically, musically, and inspiring to us all. Bill Ludwig called Bobby the fireman of percussion- racing from one instrument to another; timpani to vibes to snare to bass drum.

"Mike Balter tells me there was one particular occasion when our honoree had to use an unusual performing technique in order to cover a bass drum part. It seems that Bobby was playing with the Dick Schory Percussion Pops Orchestra. They used to set up on two different sides of the stage. On this infamous occasion, instead of going to the left, Bobby went to the right. The music called for a solo bass drum note, on count 4- but there was no bass drum on that side. So Bobby threw the beater all the way across the stage, striking the head exactly on count four! When asked later 'how did you do that?', Bobby replied "I can't give away ALL of my tricks!" (laughter, applause)

"This, as you can see, is an example of Bobby's lighthearted side. He has a wonderful sense of humor, is known by all as a caring and selfless teacher- the kind that we should all go to regularly for a tune-up. Today, Bobby continues to devote his life to sharing his vast experience and talents with all of us. He has equally inspired us with his devotion and example that he has placed as a family man"

Bobby enjoyed a close working relationship with Maurie for many years. They were on staff together at WBBM (above), and in later years Bobby not only maintained a studio at Franks, but gave clinics (below)

JIM CHAPIN CLINIC DAY AT FRANKS

(L to R) Phil Stanger, Jim Chapin, Maurie Lishon, and Bill LaCombe
Stanger had a teaching studio in Franks at the time, LaCombe was the Sonor representative.
Bill LaCombe's wife "Sis" is the daughter of Howard Emrie, (Amrawco). Her first husband was Dick Craft who passed away at a young age.

Son Marty Lishon is also an excellent conga player. Here he joins Slingerland clinicians Alex Acuna (left) and Don Alias (right) in a 1978 clinic jam.

The beginnings of the Percussive Arts Society.......

Maurie:
"The Percussive Arts Society, when it was first formed, had many of the early meetings at Frank's Drum Shop after 6 o'clock when we closed. All the guys would come up and we'd have our meetings there. We used to get into some very intereting and violent arguments....   PAS became the biggest factor of it's kind in the percussion world. Today it's THE biggest and we feel that we are responsible in many ways for the early days. Carroll Bratman, Bob Yeager, and I subsidized it the first couple of years before all the other guys got really involved financially. They jumped on the bandwagon because it was the coming thing. I served on the Board of Directors as Instrument Specialist for over ten years.

The future of Percussion was in the education of it, and that was my business axiom. That's why Janice and I got so very deeply involved in the educational processes of percussion and the percussion music and percussion teaching. We wound up with 4 studios."   (For a number of years these studios were occupied by Bob Tilles, Roy Knapp, Bobby Christian, Phil Stanger, and Jim Ross, Sr.)

Chapter Eight   Roy C Knapp

Jerry Knapp was a theater owner in Waterloo Iowa in the days of silent films. Life for Jerry and his family would no doubt have been very different if he had listened to Cecil B DeMille when DeMille came to him seeking capital-DeMille wanted Knapp to put up $5,000.00 to help him get started in film production. Knapp felt that DeMille's plans were a little too speculative, and politely declined any involvement.

Jerry's son Roy was born in 1891. As a youngster, Roy received training on mandolin, violin, and piano in addition to percussion instruments. As soon as he was old enough, Roy began to play in his father's theaters. Theater drumming in those days meant that you (along with a singer and a piano player) had to produce as many of the sounds as possible that were missing from the 'silent' films. One of the singers that Roy worked with in his father's theaters was Judy Garland's father Frank Gumm.

By the time Roy Knapp made it to Chicago in 1921 he was already a highly respected drummer and xylophone soloist. He specialized in theater work, though he had spent time with the Symphonies of Duluth and Minneapolis before moving to Chicago.

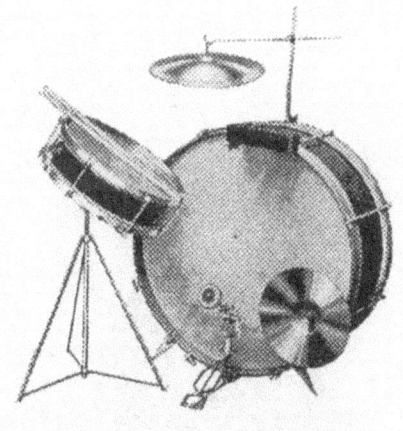

There was plenty of theater work available when Roy Knapp came to Chicago. He once said* that in 1921 there were 17 legitimate theaters in the Loop alone. "And that doesn't include moving picture shows", he reported, "but theaters running musical shows, dramas, and comedies. All of them had big orchestras. There was a lot of work for musicians back then."

*Chicago Tribune interview w/ Don DeMichael, 1978

ROY KNAPP WITH HIS 30'S-VINTAGE THEATER OUTFIT

Knapp first met Gene Krupa in 1926. "I was playing at the Capital Theater at 79th and Halsted," Knapp recalled, "One day between shows, I was downstairs in the musicians' room when the doorman called down to me. 'Hey! There's a maniac up here who wants to see you!' I went up and there was Gene and his sister. He had a pair of timpani sticks in his hand and he was beating on the walls, the chairs, his belly... everything. Now, Gene turned out to be a very gentle man; but at that time he was, well, a little bit wild. He was only 16.

"He wanted to study timpani, but I talked him into studying drums, even though he though he was already a helluva drummer.

"He was a beautiful student, the greatest talent I ever had to work with. He'd get what I was giving him almost while he was sitting there taking his lesson. He had a great sense of rhythm, of course, and it was easy for him to get the time-counting system I gave him."

In his typically humble manner, Knapp later would credit Krupa with being the one to bring honor to the drumming profession. "We were the scum of the earth. The leaders, the conductors, and most musicians had no regard for drummers. And most drummers were not musicians in the early days. There weren't half a dozen in the country who could read a bell part. They weren't trained. There were a lot of names drummers were called. Krupa changed all that. He gave us dignity."

It certainly cannot be argued that Gene Krupa changed the way the general public thought of drummers, but Knapp himself made immeasurable contributions in elevating the level of professionalism among drummers. He felt strongly that drummers serious about their craft should become total percussionists with reading skills and a knowledge of harmony.

Another big name who studied with Knapp in the early years was Sid Catlett, who took lessons in the early '30's. According to Knapp, both Dodds and Catlett were no novices... "You didn't teach those guys drums. They were already great. We were stealing what they were doing, their styles. I only helped them get a better roll. They both wanted to learn to read, and I helped them to some degree."

Another player that Knapp learned some things from was Louie Bellson. Bellson started his four years of studying with Knapp at the age of 16. Years later, according to Knapp, "Every time he came to town after he got with all those good bands like Duke Ellington and Harry James, he'd come to my studios for a lesson. I told him 'I should be taking lessons from you!', so we traded lessons. Krupa the same way. I got more out of them than they got out of me, believe me! They had more to offer- the modern stuff, y'see!"

**LOUIE BELLSON IN HIS TEENS,
WHEN HE WAS DRIVING THE WIDTH OF
ILLINOIS WEEKLY TO STUDY WITH KNAPP**

Knapp worked at keeping 'up to date' with current musical styles. "I love jazz," he told DeMichael, "I used to go hear King Oliver at the Lincoln Gardens back in 1922. I used to live there. The Friar's Inn, where the New Orleans Rhythm Kings played, the Grand Terrace when Earl Hines was there.... I lived in those places. I had to. I was a teacher, and I had to teach my kids the new styles."

Knapp taught in a tiny room at the Dixie Music House. According to Maurie (who took lessons from Roy at the Dixie) the room was barely big enough for the student, the teacher, two practice pads, and a tiny shelf-type table used for writing. Sometimes Knapp would give the student a writing exercise, then excuse himself to step out for a drink at the pub downstairs. Maurie always felt that Knapp's exiting flatulance was done deliberately to make the student work fast to earn his way out of the poorly ventilated room.

Fred Miller (left), national sales manager for the Ludwig Drum Company at the time, with Roy Knapp in the pub. Note Knapp's cigar. Though he was seldom seen without the stogie, it was practically never lit-he chewed them down. Phil Stanger recalls that there were always two or three pouches of Beech-Nut chewing tobacco on his large floor tom on the gig.

**IN 1933 KNAPP HELPED ORGANIZE NARD
THE NATIONAL ASSOCIATION OF RUDIMENTAL DRUMMERS**

NARD FOUNDERS: Front row, left to right: Harry Thompson, George A Robertson, Bill Flowers, Bill Kiefer, Bill Hammond, Joe Hathaway, Laurence Stone, Roy Knapp. Back Row: Wm F Ludwig Sr, Heinie Gerlach, Burns Moore, Billy Miller, Ed Straight

After the Dixie burned, Knapp (with the help of his wife Betty) opened the Roy C Knapp School of Percussion in Kimball Hall at Jackson Blvd and Wabash (1938). The training that this school offered was not available at even the largest universities. This fact (and the quality of the training) brought a tremendous amount of respect in a relatively short time.

College music departments at that time did not allow students to major in percussion- a situation that aggravated Knapp. Eventually he was able to help bring about a congressional hearing where he testified strenuously in favor of opening college doors to percussion majors. He was strongly opposed by heads of college music departments. According to Knapp, it took Presidential intervention on the part of Harry Truman to fix the situation. "He couldn't believe that they didn't have percussion in the colleges," Knapp said, "He put pressure on the colleges, using discrimination as the reason. That's when percussion as a major was born in every college in the United States."

By 1946 Knapp's drum school was fully accredited and offered fully transferable college credits in the study of percussion. Son Don laughingly points out that this was an especially impressive accomplishment for Roy, who didn't graduate from college or high school. He's not even sure his dad made it through grammar school! Course offerings were not limited strictly to percussion, but extended to many related fields such as theory, harmony, piano, and dancing.

At it's peak Knapp's school had 22 teachers and over 500 students. The teaching staff included Bob Tilles, Bob Seaman, Hugh Anderson, and Jose Bethancourt among others.

Hal Blaine remembers (in his book 'Hal Blaine And The Wrecking Crew') that there were even quite a few boxers enrolled, to study independant coordination. This was the latest thing for a drummer to study, and the fighters were utilizing it to learn how to throw a punch while stepping back or getting the next hand ready to throw.

Many of the students in the late '40's were there courtesy of Uncle Sam; the G.I. Bill paid the tuition for untold numbers of students. Blaine was among that group. He was just turning 20 in 1949 when he moved to Chicago to study at the Knapp school. The G.I. Bill enabled him to take a full curriculum; he was busy from 8 a.m. to 5 p.m. with a lunch break.

Hal Blaine went on to become the prototypical L.A. Studio drummer. Over 25 years he recorded nearly 35,000 tracks which included more than 40 Number One and 350 Top Ten records!

A facet of the training at the Knapp School that Blaine feels was particularly valuable was the reading. Much of the reading training was picked up through experience... Roy's son Don got to know Hal and started sending him on some of his lesser jobs.

It was about this time that Don Knapp played his first big show; the original 'Guys And Dolls' from 1950 to 1952. This launched a career which had him on the road most of the time as he toured with 'Can Can', 'Cabaret', and 'West Side Story'. Add to those credits his stints with the Ice Capades, the Ringling Brothers Circus, and the Sauter-Finnigan band, and you have a very impressive resume! Don's last show was 'Annie'. At this writing (1993) he has recently won an election and, at the age of 73, is starting a whole new career, as the president of the Chicago Federation of Musicians.

One former student of the Knapp School of Drumming whom Don is proud to have had a hand in 'career boosting' is Mel Torme. While Mel was a young teenager, Mel's father brought him to Don one day explaining that his son had a song in his head. He could get the melody down, but needed an arrangement. Don suggested he go see the piano player at the Palmer House, Ed Holtz. Holtz wrote the arrangement for the song "Lament To Love" which was a tremendous hit. (According to Don, Mel was a very fine be-bop drummer.)

Mel Torme with his first set of drums. His grandmother bought them at Frank's!

Roy Knapp was a little choosy about his students. According to Phil Stanger, Roy would start his students out on a practice drum he fabricated out of an ashtray, a couple square pieces of wood, four bolts, and a piece of timpany head. If after 3 or 4 lessons the student hadn't learned to perform a satisfactory roll on that drum, he was shipped out to one of the other teachers (Stanger mentions that this would have been Irv Hansa, Clarence Carlson, or one of the other guys.). Those who DID make the grade and were allowed to study with 'The Old Man' embarked on an unforgettable adventure. Knapp taught his students what they needed to know, though his methods were sometimes rather extraordinary. Though Knapp had a keen sense of humor, it was rather dry and it was sometimes difficult to tell whether this man with the bulldog expression was about to crack wise or give a sarcastic come-uppance.

Stanger recalls that most kids who started with Roy didn't make the cut. "First of all, he was a very BIG man. Here you have this little kid... You would never look at him- I know when I was a little kid I was afraid to look at him- it was like the wicked witch of the west! And the WORST thing that could happen would be that he would go to the phone. He'd pick it up... I'd look, and he'd start dialing my mother's number. That meant I hadn't done something- extremely bad!

"Once I came totally unprepared. He sent me to the back room, telling me 'Since you didn't do it at home, you'll do it here.' Yes, Mr Knapp. (I wasn't old enough to say 'Roy' yet- the older guys could call him Roy.) My lesson had been scheduled for 10:30 in the morning, so that was about when he started me practicing in the back room. At about one o'clock he looked in on me. He listened for a moment, and nodded. Then he reached in his pocket and gave me two dollars. He said 'Go downstairs and get me two black coffees. And a hamburger. And a milk.' I was kind of wondering whether he was going to eat all that when he continued 'You're going to get the hamburger and the milk, the coffees are for me.'

"As soon as he saw I was finished, he started me practicing again.
'Don't worry about your mother', he told me. About five o'clock he came in again. He listened, nodded, and reached in his pocket again. This time he said to get two large coffees for him and told me to get myself a piece of pie, and come back up. Now this was on a Saturday, so he had to play that night at the National Barn Dance. I finished the pie and practiced about another half hour before he called me in.
'The next time you don't come here prepared, you don't come. That's it- you're finished.'

Stanger:

"That was the most scary thing that ever happened to me in my whole life. And that includes going through a whole war! That was the ultimate putdown, that you'd get kicked out and sent home not to return. But if you look at the list of his students- those are all winners. Almost everybody there who made it- at one time or another sat in that chair."

Knapp always started the students with the snare drum (practice pad). If you lasted with him, though, it wasn't long before you started getting into scales, chords, and intervals. Stanger: "Then go down the hall and get the bucket. Fill it with water. Come back up here and go in the back room." 'What's in the back room?' "Start washing tympani heads." These were calfskin timpani heads that had to be washed down every day to bring back the collar. "He wouldn't let you PLAY them- you just washed them down, then you'd get to watch HIM play them." In one way, a lesson from 'The Old Man' was like an appointment with the doctor; you had to be there at the appointed time, but that did not mean you would start your lesson then. Lessons did not end because the clock said it was time- they ended when he was done teaching. Sometimes this meant that at the end of the day there were several students backed up still waiting for their lessons! (In later years, Maurie had to give Roy a key to the shop because he was frequently teaching after hours.)

Roy had not given up his performing career when he opened the school. He sat in the drum chair at the 'National Barn Dance' broadcasts (WLS) for 31 years! He retired from playing professionally in 1960.

By the time of his retirement from performing, activity at the drum school had slackened tremendously. 'Show' drumming and the gigs that called for multifaceted percussionists were down. Rock and Roll was starting to explode, but it was not filling the drum school with students wanting formal training. Student enrollment was down, and the teaching staff had been reduced drastically. Knapp's picture no longer adorned the drum manufacturers' catalogs and promotional literature.

This situation, combined with a couple of unscrupulous employees who were pocketing much of the cash that students paid for sticks and pads, etc. gradually led to a financial squeeze. Knapp's overdue balance with his main supplier, the Ludwig Company, grew to over a thousand dollars. A competitor of Franks Drum Shop had offered to pay Ludwig off for Knapp if he would come and teach in their shop, but Knapp was reluctant to accept the offer, which also involved selling his name.

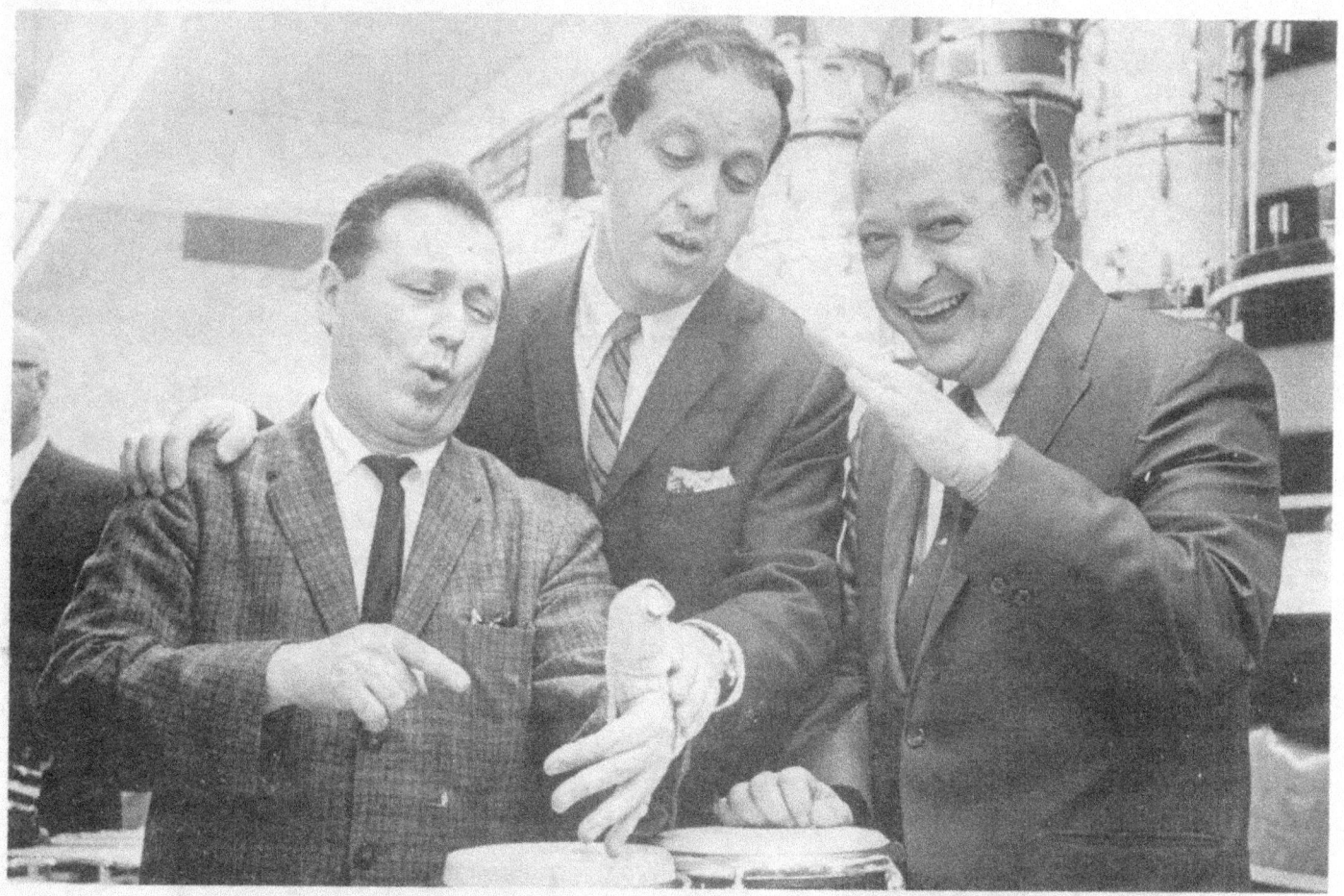

MAURIE, BOBBY ROSENGARDEN (Center), and LOU SINGER

It was during this visit (on a Rosengarden clinic day) that Bobby and Lou 'cornered' Maurie and convinced him that he was the only one who could salvage Roy's career by getting him into Franks.

Jo Jones, Frank Ippolito, and Roy Knapp, who had just received Ippolito's annual 'Gene Krupa' award.

While visiting Chicago, Bobby Rosengarden (based in New York) and Lou Singer (doing studio work in L.A.) made the obligatory visit to their mentor, finding him rather depressed about the whole situation. They went together to talk to Maurie about it. Maurie at the time was doing some remodeling; he was putting in a couple small studios and making himself a nice new office.

After the visit from Rosengarden and Singer, Maurie went to Roy and told him he'd like some help designing a teaching studio. He showed him the floor plan for what was originally going to be Maurie's new office. Roy, without knowing it, designed his own new studio. When it was ready, Maurie and Jan informed Roy he was moving in with them. They not only needed a teacher of his caliber, but also needed an educational consultant; someone to help Jan build the library, and to help with the neverending stream of questions from other teachers, performers, and students. (Knapp constantly received phone calls from all over the country with sticking questions, etc.) Maurie gave Roy a check for 1,100.00 when he moved in, because he knew about the problem with Ludwig. The check was never cashed.

The first Percussive Arts Society Hall of Fame inductees (1973). Roy Knapp (left), Haskell Harr (center) and Wm. F Ludwig Sr. (right). Also inducted, but not pictured, were John Noonan and Saul Goodman. Maurie accepted the award on behalf of Goodman, who was unable to attend.

While Knapp was grateful for the awards which formally recognized his contributions his real reward was seeing the success of his students. Many of his successful students never took time to save clippings about themselves. Recognizing this, Knapp saved every clipping he saw which related to one of his students. He made up many scrapbooks, presenting them to the students.

The following message was typed at the top of the list of Knapp's students which appears in the appendix of this book:

IN LOVING MEMORY
STUDENTS OF ROY KNAPP

As recognized artists, percussionists, teachers, and musicians, I salute you, my beloved students, for your life time of success in performance. I extend my gratitude for your complete dedication, integrity and devotion and am deeply grateful of the respect and loyal friendships we have shared through the years. Your continued success has given me the recognition I cherish today as a teacher of percussion instruments and music theory, and I am highly honored to have had you as students and my life time loyal friends.

May God Bless You
With Love,
Roy C Knapp

Roy Knapp passed away on June 17th, 1979. He taught until his death, though he was down to just a co students who came to his apartment at 29 E Oak St. Maurie was at the hospital with Don when Roy passed

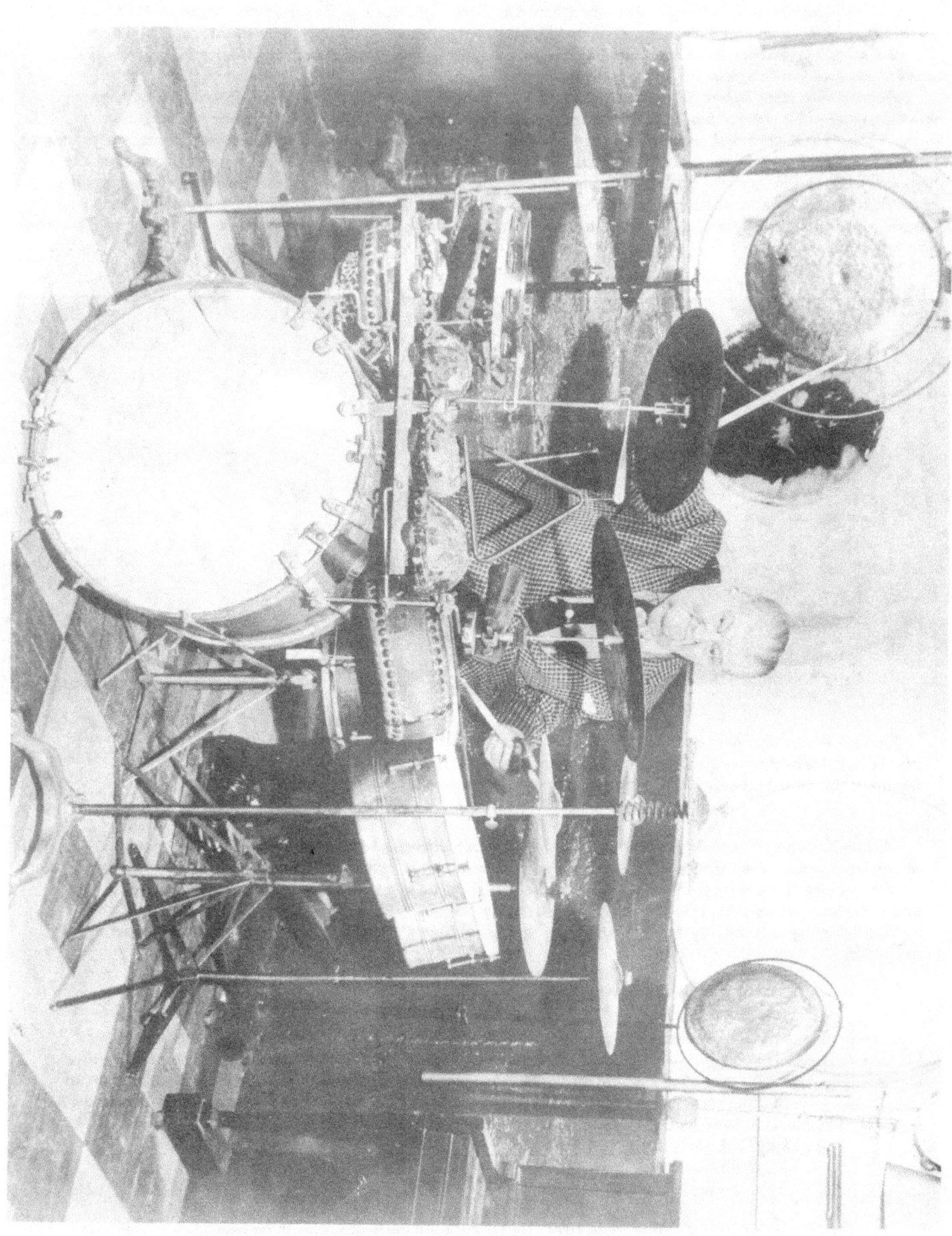

Chapter Nine
Krupa, Rich, & Bellson

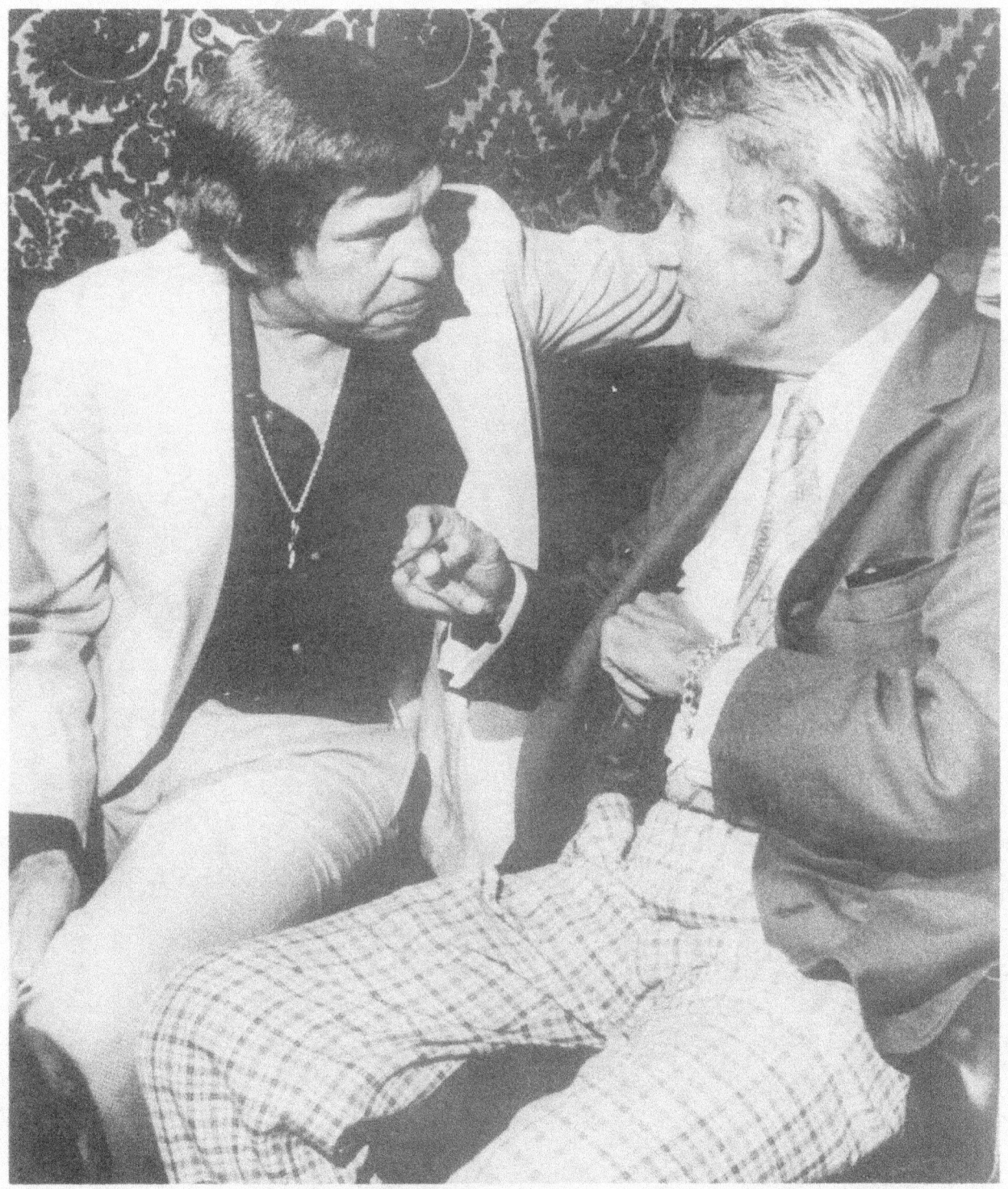

BUDDY AND GENE, SHORTLY BEFORE KRUPA'S DEATH IN 1974

While Buddy Rich is often referred to as the 'World's Greatest Drummer', there is little question that the man who really made a solo instrument of the drum set and brought drummers into the limelight was Gene Krupa. According to Buddy, "Gene Krupa was an inspiration to every big-band drummer of our time."

Before he started taking lessons from Roy Knapp at 16 (see previous chapter), Krupa had already established a relationship with Frank Gault at Dixie Music House. Frank sold Gene his first drum!

As Roy knapp mentioned, Krupa was a quick study. Eager to learn, he did not hesitate to ask other drummers about how they played certain licks. Krupa studied tympani with Saul Goodman (above and below), contributing to his melodic approach to the drum set.

KRUPA CLINIC AT FRANKS
January 29th, 1967

By the time Maurie bought Frank's in 1959, Krupa had not lived in Chicago for a number of years. He came to Chicago frequently, however, performing with orchestras and making personal appearances. His clinics were always packed; the only advertising required was word-of-mouth.

Drum duet at a NAMM (National Association of Music Merchants) convention in Chicago. Krupa and Don Osborne Jr, whose father was president of Slingerland at the time.
(Don Jr. proceeded to carve himself a successful drumming career, most notably as Mel Torme's drummer. He's been with Torme since late 1974.)

Krupa was Slingerland's #1 endorsee for over 30 years! According to Bill Ludwig Jr, it was happenstance that Slingerland landed Krupa. Krupa had played Ludwig drums as a student at Austin High School. Immediately after Krupa's gig at Chicago's Congress Hotel in 1936 (with Benny Goodman; a gig that more than any before served to catapult Krupa to superstar status) Krupa's father called the Ludwig & Ludwig sales office about an endorsement arrangement. Sales manager Fred Miller didn't have the authority to make such a deal, and referred Krupa to the head office in Elkhart.

Krupa's father flipped through the yellow pages and found the Slingerland Banjo and Drum Company. Gene was reluctant to even talk to banjo people about new drums, but his dad talked H.H. Slingerland into selling them a set wholesale.

Krupa's picture was on the cover of the next Slingerland catalog, and continued to appear on the cover of every Slingerland catalog through 1968.

Jo Jones presenting Frank Ippolito's (Professional Percussion Center, New York) first annual Gene Krupa award. This presentation, at the Newport Jazz Festival, was just four months before Krupa's death in October of 1973. In December, Ippolito wrote to Maurie, sending him copies of this picture and asking for suggestions on how to set up the voting procedure for future awards.

Buddy & Lou's party for Gene

According to Don Osborne Sr. (on left, with Gene Krupa in center and Buddy Rich on right), in the note he sent with his 1973 Christmas cards which featured this picture, this was one of the last pictures taken of Gene Krupa. The occasion was the dinner Maurie tells about-

"When Gene was getting real sick with Leukemia, Buddy and Louie Bellson got together and said they'd have a little party for him. It was held at a restaurant in New York; there were about 35 of us. Buddy and Louie were going to run this little dinner for him, but at the last minute Louie got a booking for his band in Philadelphia, so Buddy went ahead and ran the party. It was a wonderful party; you can see who was there- Zutty Singleton, Joe Morello, Sonny Igoe, etc..."

(below; Maurie and Jerry Lewis)
(below right; Armand Zildjian, Buddy, and Maurie)

Buddy & Lou's party for Gene

MARSH'S RESTAURANT, NEW YORK CITY

WEDNESDAY AUGUST 15, 1973

GENE KRUPA WITH ROY KNAPP

Front: Cliff Leeman. Behind Cliff are Frank Ippolito and Maurie Lishon.
Across back row: Sonny Igoe, Mrs. Zutty Singleton, Zutty Singleton, Krupa, Roy Knapp, Buddy Rich
(girl in front of Buddy is daughter Kathy)

As it was for many other road musicians, Frank's was a hangout for Buddy when he came to Chicago. Jan Lishon tells about an impromptu Buddy Rich 'clinic'-

"One day Chuck came to the back of the shop and said he'd just gotten a call from Buddy, who said he was coming over. Chuck said he was going to get down a drum set and set it up in case Buddy felt like playing a little.

A little while later Buddy came in, and within an hour you'd have thought we had done lots of advertising for Buddy's appearance! It was unbelievable how many drummers came from nowhere! You never would have known that we were in such a location, on the fourth floor you had to take an elevator up to! Buddy started to play a little, and the crowd continued to grow. Buddy was very congenial about this unexpected demand on his time- he played and played! This wasn't a paying performance, but he knew he was playing for appreciative fellow drummers, and he gave it his all. I could see that he was really sweating- he'd soaked completely through the sport shirt he was wearing. I got on the phone to a friend of mine who owned a nice men's clothing shop down the street, and asked her to rush over half a dozen of their best sport shirts. I figured this was the least we could do in appreciation of Buddy's generous gesture. Buddy finally wound things down, and we ushered him back to the office so the crowd would break up. As he was toweling down, I started to give the shirts to his valet. Buddy wanted to know what was going on. I explained that we wanted to give him the shirts to thank him. He took one shirt, and said he could only wear one shirt at a time. Looking at his valet, he told him not to touch the other five."

(L to R) Chuck Lishon, Jan Lishon, Buddy Rich, Suzanne Lishon, Maurie Lishon, 1967

FRANKS DRUM SHOP SELECTED AS VENUE FOR BUDDY RICH PLAYBOY POLL AWARD PRESENTATION

This photo and the accompanying writeup appeared in "The Chicagotown News" in 1967. Maurie wrote up the press release, which was printed exactly the way he wrote it up.

Maurie Lishon did it again!! He attracted a capacity crowd of almost 400 enthusiasts to FRANK'S DRUM SHOP on Saturday, October 28, to see the Fabulous **Buddy Rich** in a drum seminar and clinic, which still has Wabash Ave. agog!

The drumming sensation of the century amazed the audience with a playing performance which was sensational from start to finish, and conducted a question and answer seminar which was an educational revelation.

An added feature was the appearance of **Bobby Rosengarden**, Johnny Carson's featured drummer on the TONIGHT Show, who participated in the clinic, and shared honors with **Stan Amber** of Playboy Enterprises in presenting the coveted Playboy Award Medal to Buddy Rich, who was chosen as the top "musician's musician" in the annual Playboy poll.

The clinic marked another successful episode in the long series of free educational programs that FRANKS DRUM SHOP has been sponsoring for many years. They were inaugurated about 8 years ago to expose the younger players to good percussion.

Maurie Lishon, staff drummer at CBS-WBBM for 18 years, is currently planning another series of percussion clinics for 1968, all of which will be free to the public.

GATHERED FOR THE BUDDY RICH PLAYBOY POLL AWARD PRESENTATION

(from left) Dick Craft (Amrawco), Jose Bethancourt, Roy Knapp, Bobby Rosengarden, Buddy Rich, Maurie Lishon, Chuck Lishon, Stan Amber (Playboy Magazine), Frank Ippolito

BUDDY RICH AND HENRY ADLER, with a Henry Adler practice pad on a Slingerland 'Buddy Rich' model 4"x14" snare drum. This drum was only catalogued by Slingerland for about 3 years, from 1971 through 1973.

Louie Bellson

Maurie:
"I worked a club called "The Hi-Hat" on the swing night once or twice a week. They had a girl working there named DeeDee Bellson. She told me about this kid brother of hers who was a sensational drummer. Then I found out that he was studying with Roy Knapp, too- at the same time I was."

DeeDee Bellson went on to work for Arthur Murray as a dance teacher. Eventually the Murray Studios transferred her to Florida, where she taught for years.

Mary Selhost (Louie's sister):
"It winning that contest that really started Louie's career off. He joined Ted Fio Rito's band at seventeen- right out of high school!"

Drummers! ENTER GENE KRUPA'S NATIONAL AMATEUR SWING DRUMMERS' CONTEST!

(18 years old or under)

HERE'S a golden opportunity for the young drummers of America. The nation's No. 1 drummer, Gene Krupa, offers you:

1. A chance to win the National Amateur Swing Drummers' contest.

2. Any one of scores of fine prizes, including complete sets of the famous Slingerland "Radio King" drums.

3. A trip to New York City, with all expenses paid, for the winners who compete in the finals.

4. National publicity for you and a real chance to get started on the road to success!

It's Easy

... to enter Gene Krupa's National Amateur Swing Drum Contest, and it costs you nothing. The only requisite is that you are an amateur swing drummer, 18 years old or under.

There will be a local, regional, and a final national contest where the King of young swing drummers will be crowned! Literally thousands of dollars worth of the finest SLINGERLAND drums will be given as prizes. Who knows—this may mean a national championship, a wonderful prize, and a flying start on a professional career for you!

So don't delay a moment. The contest starts immediately. Take the coupon to your nearest Slingerland dealer today.

"4 out of 5 of the world's greatest drummers play Slingerlands!"

Sponsored by:

SLINGERLAND DRUM CO.
1335 Belden Ave.   Chicago, Ill.

Take this to your nearest Slingerland dealer who will give you complete information.

Mr. Dealer:

Please enter the bearer in Gene Krupa's National Amateur Swing Drummers' Contest, which is sponsored by the Slingerland Drum Company.

Name

Address

City   State

I am   years old.

Louie conducted many clinics at Franks over the years, beginning in Maurie's earliest days at the shop, when Louie was a Rogers endorsee.

LOUIE AT FRANKS IN THE 70'S

Chapter Ten - The Second Time Around

MAURIE "RETIRES"

"In 1974 I had heart surgery (3 bypasses) and was told I could no longer take the Chicago winters nor contend with the responsibility of operating Franks Drum Shop. I finally sold the shop to my second son, Marty, in 1978 after four years of semi-absentee management attempt."

Within a few years, Marty was forced into bankruptcy. In retrospect, he feels that the reasons for the failure of the shop break down into several categories....

First of all, there was a sense of passing of 'the old guard' - the days of all the great old jazz names hanging out at the shop were no more. This was true not only at Franks, but for the other two big shops as well; Ippolito and Yeager both died (though Yeager's shop continued to operate).

Marty does not feel that the increase in discount mail-order operations affected sales at Franks near the end nearly as much as the loss of sales due to the endorsee situation getting out of hand. Back in the days when Maurie was an endorsee, the endorsees were happy to get their pictures taken for the exposure it provided. In the seventies, however, the endorsement situation got totally out of hand. It escalated from simply getting free equipment to large cash payments and/or guarantees of high-paying clinics. One big-name drummer was signed for ten thousand dollars per year plus a guarantee of at least a dozen clinics paying $500.00 each PLUS he had at least six drum sets at all times; broadcast studio, recording studio, Vegas, and several on the road to clinics. This type of situation made it difficult to SELL equipment to these drummers. "It was losing the sales to the big guys that really hurt," says Marty. "I used to work with ALL the big guys- I sold stuff to everyone from the Stones to the Dead- my customer list included every major group in Frisco, London, New York, you name it."

Maurie adds "After they started getting all their equipment free, some of these guys would even come in the shop and ask to take stuff on account, wanting to pay it back with the free gear when it came to them."

Adding to the financial strain was a downturn in institutional sales due to tighter budgets in public schools and Universities.

After the shop went down, Marty got involved in the equipment rental business in Chicago, then into production. He was very active in Chicago-area productions such as Chicago-Fest and the Chicago Blues Festival. He then went to California to do similar work with Keith Knudsen's production company "Southern Pacific". He found his calling with concert production and has pretty much called the road home ever since; producing acts for cruise lines, traveling with touring acts, etc.

Marty with Mike Love at a Beach Boys venue; he was road manager for the group in the mid to late 80's.

During his days at Franks, Maurie gave out many copies of a transcribed Paul Gibson broadcast:

STAY YOUNG

YOUTH IS NOT A TIME OF LIFE - IT IS A STATE OF MIND It is a temper of the will, a quality of the imagination, a vigor of the emotions, a predominance of courage over timidity, of the appetite for adventure over love of ease.

NOBODY GROWS OLD BY MERELY LIVING A NUMBER OF YEARS, people grow old by deserting their ideals. Years wrinkle the skin, but to give up enthusiasm, wrinkles the soul.

Worry, Doubt, Self-distrust, Fear and Despair - these are the long, long years that bow the head and turn the growing spirit back to dust.

Whether seventy or sixteen, there is in every being's heart the love of wonder, the sweet amazement at the stars and starlike things and thoughts, the undaunted challenge of events, the unfailing childlike appetite for what next, and the joy and the game of life.

You are as young as your faith, as old as your doubt, as young as your self-confidence, as old as your fear, as young as your hope, as old as your despair.

So long as your heart receives messages of beauty, cheer, courage, grandeur and power from the earth, and from the Infinite, - so long are you young.

As broadcast by Paul Gibson, January 17, 1956

It is obvious that the lines of that broadcast struck a real chord with Maurie.... He wasn't in Florida long before he was behind the drums again. The band "Second Time Around" is made up of all ex-pros with credentials from some of the biggest name bands of the past. The band was formed in 1980 and within ten years had over 600 radio stations playing cuts from their albums. Their recordings are played all over the world. The band has a number of recordings out, and is booked months in advance. They regularly play to standing-room-only crowds, and have been featured on a special segment produced by CBS News. "Home base" for the STA can probably most accurately be defined as the Boynton Beach Civic Center. Though the Center's capacity is normally rated at 400, it is cut to 240 when STA performs. "That's the fire code", explains Parks and Recreation supervisor Sharon Golden. "We can't pack them in because people love to dance to the band, and they need the room."

Maurie also keeps busy with his correspondence, and has even lectured at Palm Beach Community College.

Maurie did double duty on this gig, playing with the Dixieland Band shown here as well as the STA. This 1989 concert in Lake Worth, Florida was attended by over 10,000 people. They sold $1,300.00 worth of STA recordings.

1990 ROSTER "THE SECOND TIME AROUND"
OVER 1,000 YEARS OF MUSICAL EXPERIENCE!

VINCENT BADLE trumpet
West Palm Beach- formerly from N.Y.C. Started playing professionally at age 12. Has played with the orchestras of HARRY JAMES (2 movies), BENNY GOODMAN, VINCENT LOPEZ, RAYMOND SCOTT on the LUCKY STRIKE HIT PARADE.

HARRY BIERMAN trumpet
Delray Beach- formerly from N.Y.C. Started playing professionally in 1929, with orchestras in the Catskills- Mt Freedom, NJ, and the N.Y.C. area.

KIT STEWART song stylist
Jupiter- formerly from Connecticut. Started her singing career at age 3 with her father's big band. Attended the H. HOBBS JORDAN School of Music, N.Y.C.- singing and playing piano for TV and Radio jingles. In Florida has appeared as a "single" or with band groups at hotels/lounges in the area.

RAY HARTMAN trombone
West Palm Beach- formerly from Bloomfield, N.J. At age 10 started playing trombone. Was with the NEW JERSEY STATE OPERA 25 years. Was conductor of the BLOOMIFIELD CIVIC BAND besides "free lancing" in the N.J. and N.Y. areas.

JOE COLLINS trombone
West Palm Beach- formerly from Alexandria, VA. At 6 years old played trumpet and switched to trombone. Attended VA Polytech playing with college bands. Locally plays with SYMPHONIC BAND of the PAL BEACHES, the "OVER 40 JAZZ ENSEMBLE", and the "CONTEMPORARY BRASS"

SANFORD STURM trombone
Delray Beach- formerly from Long Island. "Sandy" is a retired school teacher. Started on trombone in High School. Played with the popular L.I. "TOWNSMEN" dance band which is now in the Naples, FL area. Also played with the NASSAU College JAZZ GROUP.

Henry Chernin bass trombone
Lake Clarke Shores- formerly from Akron, OH. Started playing professionally at age 13. Has played with the orchestras of LOUIS PANICO, TOM CHRISTIAN, LARRY CLINTON, LARRY FUNK, and CLYDE McCOY "Sugae Blues".

ED BROWN piano
Palm Springs- formerly from New London, CT. Played first professional engagement in 1919 with the SHEPARD & SWANSON orchestra. In Florida has been with the NEAL SMITH orchestra for many years.

MAURIE LISHON drums
Royal Palm Beach- formerly from Chicago. Started playing professionally in 1928. With the orchestras of RAY BLOCK, HENRI LISHON, LOU BREESE, RAMONA. Was on the CBS staff for 19 years. Percussive Arts Society hall of fame member.

IRV MANNING bass
West Palm Beach- from England and N.Y.C. In England was with the SYDNEY LIPTON orchestra. Came to the States in 1940. Played with HARRY JAMES, BENNY GOODMAN, WOODY HERMAN, EDDIE CONDON, and toured the world with the LOUIE ARMSTRONG ALL/STARS.

RALPH DE ROUSSE bass, P.R.
Delray Beach- formerly from St. Louis, Mo. Started playing piano at age 10 in order to join H.S. band. Took up bass fiddle. Played with CHARLIE AGNEW, CHARLIE FISK and many other road bands. In the 1950's was with the great DICK JUERGENS orchestra.

DAR INMAN managing director
Lantana- formerly from Highland Park, Il. Started playing professionally in 1930 (drums). Played the Chicago area with the RED HODGSON orchestra. (Red Hodgeson is the composer of "Music Goes 'Round")

ED KRAFT sound engineer
Boynton Beach- formerly from Chicago and Libertyville, Il. Ed plays piano and in the 1930's had his own successful orchestra in Chicago.

JOHN HAMEL all saxes, clarinet
West Palm Beach- formerly from Detroit. Started playing professionally in the early 1930's - with ACE BRIGODE and His Virginians and the BERNIE CUMMINS orchestra.

ERWIN MICHAEL all saxes, clarinet
Boynton Beach- formerly from Cleveland, Ohio. Started playing clarinet in 8th grade- at age 18 joined U.S. Army where he took up sax. After the service played in the orchestras of AL DONAHUE, JIMMY DORSEY, BOB CROSBY, & GUY LOMBARDO.

PAUL DINKELOO tenor sax
Delray Beach- formerly from Highland Park, Illinois. Started playing professionally in 1928 in the Chicago area. In 1936 was with the HARVEY OLSON orchestra playing aboard the Cunard White Star ocean liners.

FLORENCE SMITH tenor sax, clarinet
West Palm Beach- formerly from Pawtucket, R.I. Started playing professionally at age 12 - in the 1930's was with PHIL SPITALNY "All Girl" orchestra.

ORVO HELANDER baritone sax
Boynton Beach- formerly from Lake Forest, IL Started playing professionally 1928 in the Chicago area. Played aboard the Cunard White Star ocean liners, HARVEY OLSON orchestra (1936) and the JOHNNY GILBERT orchestra (1937).

TOMMY SMITH musical director, lead trumpet
West Palm Beach- formerly from Glasgow, Scotland. Started playing professionally at age 14. Was on staff of BBC in London and played with the TED HEATH orchestra. Here in the U.S. was with the LES ELGART orchestra on cruise ships and the JACKIE GLEASON show.

HOWARD SICKLER trumpet
Lake Worth - formerly from Rochester, N.Y. Started playing professionally in 1929. Is a music teacher. During WWII was with the U.S. NAVY BAND directed by ORRIN TUCKER.

ORDERING INFORMATION—
"SECOND TIME AROUND" RECORDINGS

1 ☐ TAPE
It's better!
The Second Time Around DANCE BAND

PROGRAM 1
THEME / GERSHWIN MEDLEY / THE BEST THINGS IN LIFE ARE FREE / I CAN'T GET STARTED / RODGERS MEDLEY / THE MAN I LOVE

PROGRAM 2
KERN MEDLEY / BODY AND SOUL / OLD AND NEW / TENDERLY / THE S.T.A. BLUES

2 ☐ TAPE
SENIORS GOLD
The Second Time Around Dance Band

PROGRAM 1
BROADWAY GOLD / LOVER'S GOLD / I WANT A GIRL / STELLA BY STARLIGHT / BEYOND THE BLUE HORIZON

PROGRAM 2
BASIN STREET BLUES / CUTE / MISTY / GERSHWIN SWINGS / MOONGLOW

3 ☐ TAPE
SENIOR PROM
THE SECOND TIME AROUND Dance Band

SIDE 1:
THE CLAPPING MEDLEY / DEEP PURPLE / 3 DANCEABLE DOLLS (MEDLEY) / WHEN IT'S SLEEPY TIME DOWN SOUTH / BIG BAND OF THE 20's (MEDLEY)

SIDE 2:
UNREQUITED LOVE (MEDLEY) / WINCHESTER CATHEDRAL / THIS IS ALL I ASK / FOR YOU - FOR ME / I SURRENDER DEAR

4 ☐ TAPE
What A Wonderful World
The Second Time Around Dance Band

SIDE A
*THE HAPPY MEDLEY / *WHAT A WONDERFUL WORLD / *SOUVENIRS (MEDLEY) / *WHISPERING / IMAGINATION

SIDE B
*DANCER'S GOLD (MEDLEY) / *YOU'VE CHANGED / *SIDE BY SIDE / *THAT OLD FEELING / ST. LOUIS BLUES
*Music arranged by Nick Nicholson

5 ☐ TAPE
♥ *Young at Heart* ♥
♥ SIDE A ♥
STATES MEDLEY ♥ MELANCHOLY BABY ♥ FOR ME AND MY GAL ♥ THE GIRL FROM IPANEMA ♥ YOU ARE TOO BEAUTIFUL ♥ I CAN'T GIVE YOU ANYTHING BUT LOVE ♥

♥ SIDE B ♥
BUSINESSMAN'S MEDLEY ♥ ROMANCE MEDLEY ♥ IT HAD TO BE YOU ♥ AIN'T MISBEHAVIN' ♥ I THOUGHT ABOUT YOU ♥ DREAM MEDLEY ♥

6 ☐ TAPE
♪ **SALUTE TO NICK** ♪

♪ SIDE A ♪
SHUFFLE RHYTHM MEDLEY ♪ I'M CONFESSIN' ♪ THERE'LL NEVER BE ANOTHER YOU ♪ LOVE IN THE 40'S MEDLEY ♪ I CONCENTRATE ON YOU ♪ JIMMY DORSEY MEDLEY ♪

♪ SIDE B ♪
OLD BLACK MAGIC / WITCHCRAFT MEDLEY ♪ IF YOU ARE BUT A DREAM ♪ BALLIN' THE JACK ♪ SEPTEMBER SONG ♪ SOON ♪ FROM THIS MOMENT ON / I'LL GO MY WAY BY MYSELF MEDLEY ♪

7 ☐ TAPE
DANCERS' PLATINUM

♫ SIDE A ♫
DANCING IN THE DARK / CHEEK TO CHEEK MEDLEY ♫ OUR LOVE IS HERE TO STAY ♫ YOUNG AT HEART ♫ DIXIE ROSES ♫ THE VERY THOUGHT OF YOU ♫ ALL THE THINGS YOU ARE

♫ SIDE B ♫
BEGIN THE BEGUINE ♫ STARDUST ♫ JUST FRIENDS ♫ LET'S DO IT ♫ I CAN'T BELIEVE THAT YOU'RE IN LOVE WITH ME ♫ DANCERS' PLATINUM.

$5.00 each

7 TAPES $30.00
(save $5.00)

— Tax Included —

POSTAGE
$1.00 for 1 tape
1.50 " 2 "
2.00 3 or more tapes

— Satisfaction Guaranteed —
order form

NAME _____
ADDRESS _____
CITY _____

GIFT from _____

POSTAGE $ _____
TOTAL $ _____

Send to
The Second Time Around
DANCE BAND
610 S BROADWAY
LANTANA FLORIDA 33462

Civic Contributions, Recognition

Maurie and Jan were active in community affairs for many years. He was a charter member of the A. G. Beth Israel Synagogue, and organizing member of the Henry Davis "400" Juniors, vice-president and chairman of the Lifschultz Youth Foundation, the Willie Shore JWV Post, and Music and Allied Arts Bnai Brith. Maurie served as president of the Bnai Brith Lodge, and was a member of the board of directors of the Sixth District Bnai Brith.

In 1975, Maurie was named 'Man Of The Year' by the Dal Segno (a professional musician's group).

In 1980, Maurie was named Mr "Big Heart" of 1980 by the Henry Davis "400", a heart research organization affiliated with Mt Sinai Hospital Medical Center in Chicago. This prestigious award is an annual event of this repsected forty-year old fund-raising group to honor an outstanding person as Mr "Big Heart" of the year.

The Henry Davis "400" serves and supports continuing advances in all aspects of heart research and has been affilated in this role for over fifty years with the Mt Sinai Medical Center.

Maurie received a citation from the State of Israel for participation with the AMLI (American Music Library For Israel) organization.

They say the greatest honor you can receive is recognition from your peers, and for percussionists the ultimate peer recognition is induction into the Percussive Arts Society Hall of Fame. In 1989 Maurie Lishon and longtime friend and associate and Bobby Christian (center) were named to the PAS Hall of Fame. The man on the left is J.C. Combs, of Wichita State University. (PAS International Convention, Nashville, 1989)

Acceptance Speech, Maurie Lishon:

"I want to thank you for bestowing this prestigious honor upon me. It means a lot to the Lishon family because percussion has been our life. As far back as I can remember, I was the kid with the drum. I started playing in the 3rd grade and played in the school orchestra for five years. My own elementary school graduation was the 10th commencement exercise I played for. I was 13 years old.

Now, here I am- 75 years old, still playing actively (or trying), in what will be my 8th decade of playing come the '90's, standing befoire my friends and colleagues receiving this most distinguished award for only doing what I loved best- percussion-and association with the great people who comprised that wonderful world of percussion.

In all those playing years, I played theatres, (including burlesque), radio and TV, recording studios, night clubs which we referred to as 'upholstered sewers' where we learned how to play a show. It's most regrettable that most all those places are no longer existant because that type of basic training is no longer available to the ambitious young player who needs the actual experience.

Percussion has given lucky me two successful careers- one as a player in Chicago and one as owner-operator of Frank's Drum Shop. There are probably hundreds of percussionists at this convention that will attest to the feeling that Jan and I tried to create- a home away from home for students, teachers, and players. Many of today's top players and educators received cooperative help of one kind or another from us during their early years on the rough road to, hopefully, a successful career in percussion.

In 1938, returning to Chicago from working the Grand Hotel on Mackinac Island, I said to my girl friend Janice Rogers; "I think I'll get married next week." She got mad as hell thinking I had found someone new. So- I proposed marriage and said "You're marrying a set of drums and me. Be good to the drums and we'll both be good to you. We've been married for 51 years!

Jan was a dancer from New York who came to Chicago to do a show for six weeks and stayed with that job for 4 years. Little did we dream that she would become the percussion literature expert that helped so many percussionists, young players, and teachers alike, for so many years. She located and stocked perrcussion literature from all over the world. Jan had a most capable assistant whose card read "Roy Knapp- Technical Advisor"! That constituted the educational image of Franks Drum Shop for years.

In all the years I had been playing, I was a customer of Frank Gault at the old Dixie Music House. When it burnt down in 1937, he opened a specialty shop- Frank's Drum Shop. I was a customer of this wonderful, dedicated man for 30 years till I bought the business in 1959. I was still on staff at CBS at the time. I promised Frank I would try to operate the shop in the same honest, sincere manner that he did all those years. I kept the name because it was so reputable.

Jan and I felt that the 'future of percussion lay in the education of percussion', so in 1960 we started presenting clinics. Soon, our clinics became nationally known. All our clinics were held on the premises at no charge to the public. We would have as many as 400-500 people standing for hours. I repeat- we never charged anyone at our clinics and presented such greats as Buddy Rich, Joe Morello, Louis Bellson, Ed Shaughnessy, Roy Burns, Jose Bethancourt, Alan Dawson, Emil Richards, Bobby Rosengarden, Gary Burton, Bobby Christian, Joe Cusatis, Fred Hinger, Lionel Hampton, Alex Acuna, Don Alias, Barret Deems, Red Norvo, Jim Chapin, and many others through the years at no charge to anyone. Today, most clinics are anywhere from $5.00 to $15.00 admission fee. (It seems that all the player-clinicians wanted to do a clinic at Frank's Drum Shop; that was the epitome!)

At this time I would like to pay tribute to two dear friends who are no longer with us. I quote verbatim from the October, 1969 issue of "The Percussionist"- 20 years ago:

"The board of directors and executive council of the Percussive Arts Society wish to sincerely thank three instrument specialists for whom this title was originally conceived. Their undying efforts to percussion and to this Society have made it possible for us to grow to our present stature. We hope these people will continue to support us as they have in the past. It is with sincerest appreciation that we thank Mr Carroll Bratman, New York City, Mr Maurie Lishon, Chicago, and Mr Bob Yeager, Hollywood, California."

At this time I know my beloved late son Chuck is waiting for the coda. I like the way he closed any function he emceed- I quote:

"My sister thanks you, my brother thanks you. My father thanks you, my mother thanks you, and I thank you for the pleasure of your company."

Franks for the memories!

Acceptance speech, Bobby Christian:

"I wish to thank all of you wonderful people. With this array of great set players, great timpany players and xylophone players, I have a few- now if I leave out any names, please forgive me! I have written just a few things here...

Of course Maurie Lishon has been my friend for many years; Tommy Thomas, and another great friend of mine is- I call him the great (everything is G!) the Great George Gaber. To me, he is just, well, great- that's all I can say about this guy! And then I have another gentleman who saved my life- Bob Spangler with the Navy band. And another great friend, and a student of mine, Johnny Lane. And another guy- about 30 years ago I was walking down Broadway and I hear this voice saying "Bobby! Bobby!"- about half a block away. I thought to myself 'who the hell is that....' I turn around, and who was it-this guy is so down to earth, it's not even funny. It was Lou Bellson!

And another great student of mine- and this guy, many people don't know it, really plays up a storm. To MY eyes, he's outstanding. Mike Balter, my student.

I had an hour speech ready for you, but I cut it down- I'm a very bad story-teller. But I want to tell this one story. Now as you know, my left ear is kind of gone, because during our sessions they wouldn't let the orchestra out of the studio. To hear the playbacks back, they'd beat these things- I don't know how many decibels. We had to stay there because if they let us go out, half the guys would get lost. They'd go to the bar and drink it up and they'd say 'hey band! let's get back and do the session!" So anyway, I have this problem. I have a neighbor who's a millionaire, he lives next door to me, and he had a very bad problem. I said "Well what are you going to do about it?" He said "You know, I can't face my work, my employees- I'm just going crazy. But I've gone to a doctor and he says it's going to cost me $32,000.00 for a hearing aid." "32 grand?" "I'm not kidding. And I'm going to do it." He went ahead and by God, he did it! He went there and he tried it out for a week and he was a different man. He put on another ten pounds, (the poor guy had been losing weight). Anyway, he went to work and he met another big executive who was having problems. The friend said "Hi, John! How are you doing?" "I'm doing just great! I hear every word you're saying!" "Really?" "Absolutely!" "Well, listen, John. What kind is it?" "It's nine-thirty." (laughter, applause)

God Bless You!

APPENDIX

The students of Roy C Knapp

THE CRADLE OF CELEBRATED  *PROFESSIONAL PERCUSSIONISTS.......*

Roy C. Knapp

40 EAST OAK
CHICAGO, ILLINOIS 60611
312/664-5524

IN LOVING MEMORY
STUDENTS OF ROY C. KNAPP

As recognized artists, percussionists, teachers and musicians, I salute you, my beloved students, for your life time of success in performance. I extend my gratitude for your complete dedication, integrity and devotion and am deeply grateful of the respect and loyal friendships we have shared through the years. Your continued success has given me the recognition I cherish today as a teacher of percussion instruments and music theory, and I am highly honored to have had you as students and my life time loyal friends.

May God Bless You
With Love,

Roy C. Knapp

THE STUDENTS" FINAL PERFORMANCE PERFORMING IN THE HOLLYWOOD-LOS ANGELES AREA

Motion Pictures, Television, Radio, Recording Studios, Symphony, Opera, Theater, Orchestras and Bands:

Anderson, Hubert	Left Chicago in the late 1960's for motion picture studios
Burton, Victor	First to leave Chicago in the 1920's for motion pictures
Jacobs, John	Second to leave Chicago in the 1930's for motion pictures
Johnson, Urban	Third to leave Chicago in the 1930's for motion pictures
Smith, Ralph	Fifth to leave Chicago in the 1960's for motion pictures
Singer, Louis	Fourth to leave Chicago in the 1950's for motion pictures

Performing in the Dance, Cafe, Night Clubs, Theaters, Recording Studios, Concert Bands, and Orchestras

Downs, Ormand	Director of his band and with name bands
Dooley, Phillip	Director of his band and with name bands
Lyman, "Abe"	Director of his band and with name bands
Pollack, "Ben"	Director of his band and father of the modern jazz band
Patten, Phillip	With name bands - Orin Tucker
Scheer, Frank	With name bands - Dick Jurgens

THE CRADLE OF CELEBRATED      *PROFESSIONAL PERCUSSIONISTS.......*

Roy C. Knapp

40 EAST OAK
CHICAGO, ILLINOIS 60611
312/664-5524

STUDENTS OF ROY C. KNAPP

PERFORMING IN THE CHICAGO AREA

Dance, Cafe, Night Clubs, Theater, Recording Studios,
Concert, Orchestras, Bands

Bills, Warren	Name Bands, his Band, Booking Agent
Brums, George	Name Bands
Boyle, Peter	Name Bands
Borden, Richard	Name Bands
Beaver, Gerry	Name Bands, in College
Bernaz, Joseph	Name Bands
Brownold, James Sr. (Retired)	Name Bands
Brownold, James Jr.	Name Bands, Teacher, Percussion, Music, Private Studio
Carlton, "Dick"	Name Bands, his Band, Booking Agent
Clair, Robert	Name Bands, Teacher, Percussion, Music, Private Studio
Corondo, Julio	Name Bands, in College
Clark, Robert	Name Bands, in College
Cyson, Larry	Name Bands, Teacher, Percussion, Music, Private Studio
Cezir, Gene	Name Bands, Teacher, Percussion, Music, Private Studio
Deems, Barret	Name Bands, Performed many Name Bands
Evans, "Chick"	Name Bands, Teacher, Percussion, Music, Private Studio
Ettleson, Steve	Name Bands, Las Vegas, Play Boy Acts
Faren, John	Name Bands, his Band
Graham, Roy Jr.	Name Bands, Organist, Vibes
Gartland, Carl	Name Bands, Actor, Model, Singer
Goshen, David	Name Bands, Teacher, Percussion, Music, Private Studio
Glander, Thomas	Name Bands
Hussen, Henry	Name Bands, Teacher, Percussion, Private, Music
Isaacs, Henry	Name Bands, his Band, Booking Agent, Studio
Jerger, "Jake"	Name Bands, Teacher, Percussion, Music, Private Studio
Jones, Robert	Name Bands, Clown, McDonald's Hamburger, Actor
Jasper, Nancy	Name Bands
Knapp, James Lee	Name Bands, Frank Sinatra, Jr., Las Vegas Show Band Acts
Kindred, Walter	Name Bands
Kaplan, Ron	Name Bands
Kussius, Harold	Name Bands, the "Old Reliable" Shows, etc.
Lewis, Eric	Name Bands, Teacher, Percussion, Music, Private Studio
Mueller, William	Name Bands, Teacher, Percussion, Music
Mariash, Max	Name Bands, Van Dam Quintette
Murray, Dennis	Name Bands, in College
Morrison, Russ	Name Bands
Larry McCormack	Name Bands, Drum Corp Specialist
Newell, Robert	Name Bands

THE CRADLE OF CELEBRATED *PROFESSIONAL PERCUSSIONISTS....*

Roy C. Knapp

40 EAST OAK
CHICAGO, ILLINOIS 60611
312/664-5524

STUDENTS OF ROY C. KNAPP

PERFORMING IN THE CHICAGO AREA

Brabec, Harry	N.B.C. Studio, Chicago; Washington Symphony, Name Bands, etc.
Bozin, William	
Budinger, Peter	N.B.C. Studio
Bever, Bruce	
Balter, Michael	Musical Shows, Recordings, Name Bands, Etc.
David Bovo	Concert Bands, Orchestras, etc.
Christian, "Bobbie"	N.B.C., C.B.S., A.B.C. Studios, N.B.C. Toscanini Symphony, his band, etc.
Dendy, Sam	Chicago, Pittsburgh Symphony, Concerts, etc.
Dean, "Samy"	Senior Citizens, Symphony, Theater, Dance, etc.
Elias, Shelly	President, Recording Studio, Musical Shows, etc.
Graham, Roy Jr.	W.G.N. Studio, Theater, Dance, etc.
Glenene, Thomas	Chicago Symphony, Theater, Concert (Retired)
Harr, Haskell	Author, Percussion Methods, Band Director, Theater (retired)
Honsa, Irving	W.L.S. Studio, Theater, Dance, etc.
Hammernick, Donald	W.G.N. Studio, Name Bands, etc.
Jensen, Pearl	Chicago Women's Symphony, Theater, Dance, etc.
Knapp, Donald	C.B.S. Studio, Chicago Lyric Opera, Theater, Musical Shows, et
Kilcran, James	Chicago Lyric Opera, Grant Park, Composer, Arranger
Kaplan, Marvin	Chicago Lyric Opera, Grant Park Symphony, Theater, Dance, etc
Ludwig, William II	Concerts, Theater, Symphony, present President, Ludwig Drum C
Lishon, Maurice	C.B.S. Studio, President, Frank's Drum Shop, Chicago
Matuszewski, Gary	
Peters, Gordon	Chicago, Rochester Philharmonic, Symphony, U.S. Military Academy Band, etc.
Pierarczy, James	Indiana Symphony, Theater, Dance, etc.
Rullo, Frank	N.B.C., A.B.C., Studio, Theater, Name Bands, etc.
Reynolds, Elenore	Chicago Woman's Symphony, Theatre, Dance, etc.
Russ, James Jr.	
Sayers, Lionel	Chicago Symphony - for many years Symphony librarian
Sedivy, Benedict	Chicago Civic Opera, Milwaukee Symphony, Ballet, etc.
Walton, Charles	
Wessberg, Robert	Director, Recording Studio
Weigman, Herman	Theater, Dance, Band Directors, etc.
Zuzanek, Norma	

THE CRADLE OF CELEBRATED  *PROFESSIONAL PERCUSSIONISTS.......*

Roy C. Knapp

40 EAST OAK
CHICAGO, ILLINOIS 60611
312/664-5524

STUDENTS OF ROY C. KNAPP

PERFORMING IN THE CHICAGO AREA

Dance, Cafe, Night Clubs, Theater, Recording Studios, Orchestras, Bands

Olliverious, Gladys	Name Bands, Night Clubs, Marimba Soloist
Olsen, Jerry	Name Bands
Riggs Guidotti, Henry	Name Bands, the "Old Reliable," Shows, etc.
Rush, Henry	Name Bands
Russell, "Hal"	Name Bands, Teacher, Percussion, Music, Private Studio
Russell, Robert	Name Bands
Russell, Connie	Name Bands
Rich, Allen	Name Bands, Night Clubs, The Rich Family Show
Siewell, "Denny"	
Jantick, George	Name Bands
Reynolds, Eleanor	Name Bands
Stanger, Phillip	Name Bands, Teacher, Percussion Music, Private Studio
Southgate, George	Name Bands, Teacher, Percussion Music, Private Studio
Stoll, Larry	Name Bands, Teacher, Percussion Music, Private Studio
Stukenberg, Ellis	Name Bands
Saunders, "Red"	Name Bands, his Band, Booking Agent
Sierzega, Glen	Name Bands
Stalik, Jerry	Name Bands
Tannenbaum, "Sammy"	
Zuzaner, Norma	Name Bands

JOBBING DRUMMERS PERFORMING WITH OTHER INTEREST

Dance, Cafe, Night Clubs, Theater, Recording Studios, Orchestras, Bands

Anderson, Donald	Honorable Judge, Kane County Courthouse, Geneva, Ill.
Arseth, Pinkey	
Acri, Robert	In college, law
Andretti, Roy	Bank
Aparo, Salvatore	In school
Alberts, Douglass	Sales
Arnt, David	Sales
Bachman, David	Painter
Berman, Louis Sr.	Accountant
Berman, Louis Jr.	In college
Bugglio, Charles	Sales
Ballou, Ray	Restaurant Owner
Bush, Vern	Advertising
Brennan, William	Night Club Owner
Crawford, Harvey	Clothing
Cletcher, John H.	Bank
Caluccio, Tony	Electrician
Corso, Rudolph	Restaurant

THE CRADLE OF CELEBRATED   PROFESSIONAL PERCUSSIONISTS.......

Roy C. Knapp

40 EAST OAK
CHICAGO, ILLINOIS 60611
312/664-5524

STUDENTS OF ROY C. KNAPP
JOBBING DRUMMERS PERFORMING - WITH OTHER INTERESTS
IN THE CHICAGO AREA
Dance, Cafe, Night Clubs, Theater, Recording Studios,
Concerts, Orchestras, Bands

Draper, Arthur	President, Real Estate, Draper & Kramer
Daner, James	Sales
Daum, Robert	Real Estate
Dillon, William	Sales
Dec, Paul	Sales
Edlemair, Joseph	In college
Florian, Ralph	Sales
Ferguson, Robert	Security
Felber, Edward	Board of Trade
Graham, Earl	Transportation
Grunditz, George	Real Estate
Galter, Jack	Real Estate
Gerlack, Richard	Sales Manager
Gill, Richard	Sales
Gilhouey, Patrick	Bank
Glerum, Glen	Accountant
Helmer, William	Accountant
Hass, Sidney	City Hall
Holden, Keith	Sales
Hartric, William	In college
Heims, William	Sales
Harding, William	Accountant
Horn, Robert	Photographer
Hawthorne, HARRY	In school — U. of Miami — Fred Wickstrom.
Jablonski, Jerry	Supervisor, Production
Judlowski, Robert	Meat salesman
Keck, Robert	Insurance
Leffler, Gerald	Sales Manager, Fuller Brush Co.
Lienweber, Paul	Sales
Mulvey, John	Airplane Travel Service
Mitterer, Ray	Public Relations
Mendell, Robert	Photographer
Migaz, Richard	IBM Computer Operator
Maxwell, Steve	Sales
Means, Chester	Railroad
Marald, John	Cafe, Night Club, Organist
Marinez, Jack	In school
Mitchell, Kenneth	In school
Novit, Jules	Bartender, Manager
Kaplan, Charles	Transportation
Botteroff, Alfred	Sales
Gross, Douglass	Transportation

THE CRADLE OF CELEBRATED   *PROFESSIONAL PERCUSSIONISTS.......*

Roy C. Knapp

40 EAST OAK
CHICAGO, ILLINOIS 60611
312/664-5524

STUDENTS OF ROY C. KNAPP

JOBBING DRUMMERS PERFORMING - WITH OTHER INTEREST IN THE CHICAGO AREA

Dance, Cafe, Night Clubs, Theater, Recording Studios, Concerts, Orchestras, Bands

Oldenberg, Frank Jr.	Bank
Peterson, Robert	Carpet
Page, William	Organ, Piano, Sales Manager
Paparocky, Ronald	School
Ratijir, Alyda	Physician
Rodriguez, Jack	Detective, Security
Robertson, Robert	Piano Tuner, Sales
Roth, Edward	Sales
Rudy, James	
Sacks, "Jackie"	Newspaper
Scherred, Jack	Booking Agent
Sunowski, Robert	Meat, Sales
Szubka, George	IBM Computer Operator
Schuman, Guy	In school
Sagrue, Brian	Printer
Spangler, Robert	Sales
Sullivan, Frank	Meat, Wholesale Owner
Saffold, Thomas	Lumber business
Tiebold, Robert	Restaurant, Real Estate
Targo, David	In school
Uram, James	Sales
Williams, "Doc"	Bank
Whitehead, Ray	Sales
Witts, Charlie	In school

PERCUSSION TEACHERS IN ROY C. KNAPP'S PERCUSSION MUSIC SCHOOL

Anderson, Hubert (Dec'd)	Knapp, Donald (son)
Anderson, Dale	Knapp, James (son)
Buggert, Robert (my first teacher)	Kilgran, James
Bethencourt, Jose (Dec'd)	Kristefek, Otto (Dec'd) Studied mallet with
Brabec, Harry	Mariash, Max R.C.K.
Carlsen, Clarence (Dec'd)	Noonan, John P. (Assoc. Director of School)
Dean, Sam	Salmon, James
Honsa, Irving (with R.C.K. 24 yrs.)	Sjoblom, Alfred
Hyams, Margerie (did not study with R.C.K.)	Tilles, Robert (Dec'd)(with R.C.K. 22 yrs.)
Voy, Tay (did not study with R.C.K.)	

THE CRADLE OF CELEBRATED   *PROFESSIONAL PERCUSSIONISTS.....*

Roy C. Knapp

40 EAST OAK
CHICAGO, ILLINOIS 60611
312/664-5524

STUDENTS OF ROY C. KNAPP

PERFORMING IN THE HOLLYWOOD-LOS ANGELES AREA

Motion Pictures, Television, Radio, Recording Studios,
Symphony, Opera, Theater, Orchestras and Bands

Anderson, Dale	Symphony, Recording, Picture Studios
Bellson, Louie	Director of his band, Picture Recording Studios
Blain, "Hal"	Director of his band, Picture Recording Studios
Cottler, "Irving"	Name bands, Studios, 25 years Frank Sinatra's Drummer
Conzelman, Robert	30 years with Columbia Studios
Flyn, Frank	Director of his band, Picture Recording Studios
Florio, Andy	Name bands, Picture Recording Studios
Ganduglio, James	Name bands, Picture Recording Studios
Holland, Milton	Name bands, Picture Recording Studios
Hobin, William	Name bands, Motion Pictures, Television Director
Jeffries, Norm	Name bands, Picture Recording Studios
Kapp, Herman	Name bands, Picture Recording Studios
Torme, "Mel"	Director of his band, Picture Studios, Singer, Composer, Studio Director

PERFORMING IN OTHER CALIFORNIA AREAS

Dance, Cafe, Night Clubs, Theater, Recording Studios,
Concert Bands, Orchestras

Berres, Ted	Sherman Oaks, name bands
Clausen, Marty	Santa Barbara, name bands
Gerace, Joseph	Santiago, name bands
Nasitir, Gerry	Oakland, name bands
Picardy, Tony	Lacanada, name bands
Thielman, August	Garden Grove, name bands
Trace, "Al"	Van Nuys, his Band, Singer, Composer
Weidon, Kenneth	Arcadia, name bands, Director of Music-Public Schools
Whitcomb	Anheim, name bands
Zinders, Earl	San Francisco, name bands, Fullbright Award, Composition

PERFORMING IN THE LAS VEGAS AREA

Casello, "Danny"	Name bands, Night Clubs, Recording Studios
Casello, "John"	Name bands, Night Clubs, Recording Studios
Howard, Smith	Name bands, Night Clubs, Recording Studios
Nasham, John	Name bands, Night Clubs, Recording Studios
Vegand, Edward	Name bands, Night Clubs, Recording Studios

THE CRADLE OF CELEBRATED PROFESSIONAL PERCUSSIONISTS.......

Roy C. Knapp

40 EAST OAK
CHICAGO, ILLINOIS 60611
312/664-5524

STUDENTS OF ROY C. KNAPP - continued

PERFORMING IN THE NEW YORK AREA

Alexandria, Mousy	Name bands, Recordings
Derrick, Frank	Name bands, Recordings, N.Y. Bubbling Brown Sugar Musical Show
Hard, Warren	Name bands, Recordings, N.Y. many Musical Shows
Rosengarden, "Bobbie"	Name bands, Recordings, N.Y. Director, his Band, Clinician, etc.
Yeager, Harry	Name bands, N.Y. many name bands, Recordings

THE CRADLE OF CELEBRATED  *PROFESSIONAL PERCUSSIONISTS.......*

Roy C. Knapp

40 EAST OAK
CHICAGO, ILLINOIS 60611
312/664-5524

STUDENTS OF ROY C. KNAPP
PERFORMING IN THE SYMPHONY, OPERA, BALLET, ORCHESTRAS

Chicago Symphony
Brabec, Harry (and Washington Symphony)
Denov, Sam (and Pittsburgh Symphony)
Graham, Allen (and Indianapolis Symphony)
Glenake, Thomas
Peters, Gordon (and Rochester Philharmonic)
Sayers, Lionel (Librarian)

Boston Symphony
Christian, "Bobbie" (NBC) Arthuro Toscanini
   Symphony
Thompson, "Tommy" (and Cincinnati Symphony)

New York Philharmonic Symphony
Layfield, Arthur (and Chicago Grand Opera)

Minneapolis Symphony
Weffling, Emil (and Detroit Symphony)

Duluth Symphony
Soderberg, Walter

Chicago Little Symphony
Mann, Ray

Grant Park Symphony
Brabec, Harry
Denov, Sam
Gordon, James
Kaplan, Marvin
Kilcran, James
Matuszewski, Gary
Peters, Gordon
Wickstrom, Fred

Waterloo Symphony
Hogancamp, Randy

Indiana Symphony
Pierarzyk, James

Foreign Country
Holland Symphony
Gordon, James

Chicago Lyric Opera
Kaplan, Marvin
Kilcran, James
Knapp, Donald (son, R.C.K.)
Kristufer, Otto (and St. Louis Symphony)
Sidivy, Benedict (and Milwaukee Symphony)

Miami Philharmonic Symphony
Wickstrom, Fred

Austin Symphony
Frock, George

Bloomington Symphony
Noonan, John

Chicago Women's Symphony (Retired)
Jackson, Margaret Resser
Nilson, Emma
Reynolds, Elenore
Wickstrom, Vera Gene
Zuzaner, Norma

Chicago Civic Symphony, Gordon Peters, Dir.
Brabec, Harry
Christian, Bobbie
Denov, Sam
Ellefsen, Arthur
Gleneke, Thomas
Gordon, James
Graham, Allen
Graham, Roy Jr.
Kaplan, Margin
Kilcran, James
Kimmey, Allen
Kussius, Harold
Ludwig, William Jr.
Matuszewski, Gerry
Peters, Gordon
Picardi, Tony
Sayer, Lionel
Tilles, Robert

THE CRADLE OF CELEBRATED  *PROFESSIONAL PERCUSSIONISTS.......*

Roy C. Knapp

40 EAST OAK
CHICAGO, ILLINOIS 60611
312/664-5524

STUDENTS OF ROY C. KNAPP

PERFORMING IN OTHER AREAS

Motion Pictures, Television, Radio, Recording Studios, Symphony, Opera, Theater Orchestras and Bands, Dance, Cafe, Night Clubs, Concerts

Buggert, Robert	DeKalb, Ill., Dean of Liberal Arts & Sciences, Northern Illinois University
Englemen, William	South Bend, Ind., Band Director, South Bend Schools
Frock, George	Austin, Texas, Director of Percussion, University of Texas, Austin Symphony
Gerdon, Thomas	Omaha, Neb., Director of Percussion, College, Omaha Symphony
Hynes, Matt	Fairfax, Va., Director of Percussion, Fairfax Schools
Hoghncamp, "Randy"	Cedar Falls, Iowa, Director of Percussion, University of No. Iowa, Symphony
Hady, Frank	Milwaukee, Wis., Director of Percussion, Milwaukee Schools
Kozak, "Eddie"	Schreveport, La., Director of Percussion, Kozak Schools, Symphony
Lefevor, Maxine	Lafayette, Ind., Director of Band, Percussion, Purdue University
Mitka, Manny	Kenosha, Wis., Director of Percussion, Kenosha Schools
Minstreta, Tony	Albera, N.M., Director of Percussion, Albera Schools
Noonhn, John P.	Normal, Ill., Director of Percussion, Wesleyan University (Ret.)
Salmon, James	Kenosha, Wis., Director of Percussion, University of Michigan (Ret.)
Soebing, Hugh	Quincy, Ill., Director of Percussion, Quincy College
Snyder, Roy	Milwaukee, Wis., Director of Percussion, Milwaukee Schools
Spain, Raymond	Ettrer, Va., Director of Percussion, Ettrer Schools
Tomas, "Tommy"	Kalamazoo, Mich., Private Studio, Percussion, Music
Werner, Otto	Ft. Collins, Col., Band Director, Colorado State University

PERFORMING IN FOREIGN COUNTRIES

Bishop, Wally	Amsterdam, Holland - Name band, Earl Hines
Gorden, James	Harlem, Holland - Tympanist, Recording
Golden, "Bobbie"	Tokyo, Japan - The Bobbie Golden Band, Concerts, Night Clubs

THE CRADLE OF CELEBRATED

PROFESSIONAL PERCUSSIONISTS....

Roy C. Knapp

40 EAST OAK
CHICAGO, ILLINOIS 60611
312/664-5524

IN LOVING MEMORY
STUDENTS OF ROY C. KNAPP

FINAL PERFORMANCE IN THE CHICAGO AREA

Motion Picture, Television, Radio, Recording Studios,
Symphony, Opera, Theaters, Dance, Orchestras and Bands

Bethen Court, Jose	NBC TV, Radio, Recording Studios
Budinger, Harry	NBC TV, Radio, Recording Studios
Chalafaux, Milton	CBS TV, Radio, Recording Studios
Graham, Roy Sr.	WGN TV, Radio, Recording Studios
Rimmey, Allen	CBS TV, Radio, Recording Studios
Krustufer, Otto	Chicago Civic Opera, St. Louis Symphony, Theater
Kelly, Jack	WCFL, Directo of his Band
Tellis, Robert	CBS, name bands
Walker, Stewart	Theater, name bands
Alvin, "Danny"	Director of his band, name bands, Recording, Theater
Arseth, "Pinkey"	Director of his band, name bands, Recording, Theater
Bertrand, James	Director of his band, name bands, Recording, Theater
Carlsen, Clarence	Director of his band, name bands, Recording, Theater
Cavalo, Patrick	Director of his band, name bands, Ice Show
Dodds, "Babie"	A Legend, First Dixieland Band in Chicago, Ring Oliver
Greenberg, Martin	Name Bands, Recording, Theater
Gowens, Estes	Name Bands, Recording, Theater
Kalabza, Joseph	Name Bands, Recording, Theater
Lennon, Ray	Name Bands, Recording, Theater
Loyd, Joseph	Name Bands, Recording, Theater
LaFrano, Tono	Name Bands, Recording, Theater
Magnus, Alfred	Name Bands, Recording, Theater
Metz, "Benny"	Name Bands, Recording, Theater
Moody, George	Name Bands, Recording, Theater
McKay, James	Name Bands, Recording, Theater
Nelson, Jacob	Name Bands, Recording, Theater
Nilson, Emma	Name Bands, Recording, Theater
Oldenberg, Frank Sr.	Name Bands, Recording, Theater
Petee, Jack	Director of his Band, name bands, Recording, Theater
Petrone, George	Director of his Band, name bands, Recording, Theater
Stevensen, Dean	Director of his Band, name bands, Recording, Theater
Waller, Al	Name Bands, Recording, Theater
Winters, Ray	Name Bands, Recording, Theater
Zipperstein, Louis	Name Bands, Recording, Theater

THE CRADLE OF CELEBRATED PROFESSIONAL PERCUSSIONISTS.......

Roy C. Knapp

40 EAST OAK
CHICAGO, ILLINOIS 60611
312/664-5524

IN LOVING MEMORY

STUDENTS OF ROY C. KNAPP
FINAL PERFORMANCE IN OTHER LOCATIONS

Motion Pictures, Television, Radio, Recording
Studios, Symphony, Opera, Theater, Orchestras
and Bands

Krupa, Gene	N.Y. City; Director of his band, name bands
Layfield, Arthur	N.Y. City, N.Y. Philharmonic Symphony, Chicago Grand Opera
Marsh, George	N.Y. City, Paul Whiteman, name bands, theater, recording
Mann, Ray	Rockford, Illinois, Chicago Little Symphony, Theater, Dance
Paulsen, William	N.Y. City, Columbia Recording Studios, Sousa and Bachman Bands
Quigley, Herbert	N.Y. City Recording Studios, Theater, Arranger, Composer
Rodriguez, "Willie"	N.Y. City Recording Studios, Paul Whiteman, name bands
Soderberg, Walter	Duluth, Minn., N.Y. City Recording Studios, Duluth Symphony, Theater
Thompson, "Tommy"	Boston, Mass., Boston and Cincinnati Symphony, Theater, Dance
Todd, Lyle	St. Petersburg, Fla., N.Y. City Rdcording Studios, A.B.C. Breakfast Club Radio Show, Theater, Dance
Weffling, Emil	Minneapolis, Minn., Minneapolis and Detroit Symphony, Theater, Dance
Wettling, George	N.Y. City Recording Studios, Paul Whiteman, many name bands

Final Performance in the Dance, Cafe, Night Clubs, Theater, Recording Studio, Bands and Orchestras

Catlett, "Sid"	N.Y. City, name bands, Louis Armstrong, famous drummer (jazz)
Carter, Donald	N.Y. City, name bands
Cearcy, Orville	N.Y. City, name bands, Raymond Scott
Cross, Ariel	Des Moines, Iowa, name bands, Drum Corp Specialist
Dreeves, Allen	Madison, Wis., name bands, Percussion Educator
Elliot, James	Miami, Fla., name bands
Elefsen, Arthur	N.Y. City, name bands, Wayne Ring
Emmerson, Howard	Minneapolis, Minn., name bands, Director of his band
Finley, Louis	Austin, Texas, name bands
Laurie, Maurie	Santingo, Fla., name bands, popular Chicago Percussionist
Mazer, James	Miami, Fla., name bands
McElroy, "Chief"	Minneapolis, Minn., name bands, Clown of Percussion
Pollack, Joseph	Indianapolis, Ind., name bands
Snyder, Frank	Phoenix, Ariz., name bands, discovered many famous musicians
Tough, Dave	N.Y. City, name bands, all of them - Goodman, etc.

THE CRADLE OF CELEBRATED

PROFESSIONAL PERCUSSIONISTS.......

Roy C. Knapp

40 EAST OAK
CHICAGO, ILLINOIS 60611
312/664-5524

STUDENTS OF ROY C. KNAPP

TEACHING IN THE HIGH SCHOOLS
DIRECTOR OF INSTRUCTION FOR THE PERCUSSION INSTRUMENTS - MUSIC
IN THE CHICAGO AREA

Brownold, James	Brookfield
Clair, Robert	Morton Grove
Cyson, Larry	Chicago
Cezik, Gene	Chicago
Dean, Sam	Hinsdale
Evans, Chick	Elmhurst York H.S.
Faren, Johnny	Oak Lawn
Husen, Henry	Chicago
Honsa, Irving	Berwyn
Jerger, "Jake"	Des Plaines
Kilcran, James	Oak Lawn
Lewis, Eric	Chicago
Morris, William	Chicago
Rullo, Frank	Elmwood Park
Stull, Larry	Chicago
Stanger, Phillip	~~Evanston~~ New Trier, Winnetka 17 yrs.
Southgate, George	Palatine
Weigman, Herman	Chicago

TEACHING IN THE HIGH SCHOOLS
OTHER LOCATIONS
DIRECTOR OF INSTRUCTION FOR THE PERCUSSION INSTRUMENTS - MUSIC

Engleman, William	South Bend, Indiana - Director of Bands
Hyns, Matt	Fairfax, Virginia
Mueller, William	Joliet, Illinois
Mitka, Manny	Kenosha, Wisconsin
Miller, Steve	Miami, Florida
Minstretta, "Tony"	Albuquerque, New Mexico
McGowan, Jeffrie	Des Moines, Iowa
Naftulin, Louis	Cleveland, Ohio
Nasitir, Gerry	Oakland, California
Snivley, "Mike"	Ft. Wayne, Indiana
Sneider, Roy	Milwaukee, Wisconsin
Vegand, Edward	Lake Tahoe, Nevada
Weidow, Kenneth	Arcadia, California, Director of Music, Public Schools

These students' names have been listed in the previous pages.

THE CRADLE OF CELEBRATED  *PROFESSIONAL PERCUSSIONISTS......*

Roy C. Knapp

40 EAST OAK
CHICAGO, ILLINOIS 60611
312/664-5524

STUDENTS OF ROY C. KNAPP

TEACHING IN COLLEGES AND UNIVERSITIES IN THE
UNITED STATES AND FOREIGN COUNTRIES

Anderson, Dale	University of Southern California, Los Angles, California
Buggert, Robert	Northern Illinois University (Dean), DeKalb, Illinois
Bellson, Louie	Clinician, Percussion Soloist
Balter, Michael	DePaul University, Chicago, Illinois
Bozin, Bill	Roosevelt University, Chicago, Illinois
Bishop	Amsterdam Music College, Amsterdam, Holland
Christian	DePaul University, Chicago, Illinois
Elias, Shelly	Triton Junior College, Maywood, Illinois
Frock, George	University of Texas, Austin, Texas
Gordon, James	Harlem University, Harlem, Holland
Gerdon, Thomas	Omaha College, Omaha, Nebraska
Harr, Haskell	Vendencoor College of Music, Chicago, Illinois
Hawthorn, Harry	Miami University, Miami, Florida
Hogancamp, "Randy"	Iowa State College, Cedar Falls, Iowa
Kozak, Eddie	Shreveport Music College, Shreveport, Louisiana
LeFevor, Maxine	Purdue University, Lafayette, Indiana
Mataszewski, Gary	Roosevelt University
Noonan, John	Illinois Wesleyan University, Bloomington, Illinois
Peters, Gordon	Northwestern University, Evanston, Illinois
Pierarzyk, James	Governors State University, Park Forest, Illinois
Rosengarden, "Bobbie"	Clinician, Percussion, Soloist, New York City, N.Y.
Salmon, James	University of Michigan, Ann Arbor, Michigan
Soebing, Hugh	Quincy University, Quincy, Illinois
Tham, Duane	Elmhurst College, Elmhurst, Illinois
Thomas, Tommy	Rollins College, Rollins, Florida
Werner, Otto	Colorado State College, Ft. Collins, Colorado
Wickstrom, "Freddie"	Miami University, Miami, Florida
Walton, Charles	Malcolm X College, Chicago, Illinois

These students have been listed in the previous pages

THE CRADLE OF CELEBRATED

PROFESSIONAL PERCUSSIONISTS.......

Roy C. Knapp

40 EAST OAK
CHICAGO, ILLINOIS 60611
312/664-5524

STUDENTS OF ROY C. KNAPP

ORCHESTRA AND BAND DIRECTORS
DIRECTING THEIR OWN ORCHESTRAS AND BANDS

Alvin, "Danny" (Dec'd)	Famous Dixieland Jazz Drummer
Arseth, "Pinkey" (Dec'd)	Society Orchestras
Bellson, Louis	Performed many famous name bands, Ellington, etc.
Blain, "Hal"	Performed many famous name bands, Ellington, etc.
Bills, Warren	Performed many famous name bands, Ellington, etc.
Baduc, Ray	The famous Ben Pollack, Bob Crosby Bands and Orchestras
Benthencourt, Jose (Dec'd)	International Marimba Bands
Christian, "Bobbie"	Paul Whiteman, many name bands and orchestras
Carlton, "Dick"	Dance, Show, Orchestras, Bands
Clairage, Gay	Dance, Show, Orchestras, Bands
Dodds, "Babie" (Dec'd)	King Oliver, Louie Armstrong, etc. (A Living Legend)
Derrick, Frank III	Bubbling Brown Sugar Musical Show, New York City
Dooley, "Phil" (Dec'd)	Dixie, Jazz, Orchestras, Name Bands
Flynn, Frank	Recording, Show, Dance, Orchestra
Featherstone, James	Dance, Show, Orchestra, Name Bands
Faren, John	Jazz, Show, Orchestra, Band
Krupa, Gene (Dec'd)	Benny Goodman, Name Bands, a Creative Genius
Kelly, Jack (Dec'd)	Radio, Theater, Name Bands, Orchestra
Lyman, "Abe" (Dec'd)	Society Dance, Show, Band, Orchestra
McElroy, (Chief) (Dec'd)	Jazz, Comedy, Band
Pollack, "Ben"	Father of modern Jazz Orchestras, Bands
Rodriguez, Willie	Paul Whiteman, Great Latin Drummer
Rosengarden, Robert	Dick Cavett, Director of Television Show, many famous Bands
Saunders, "Red"	Earl Hines, many Name Bands, Orchestras
Snyder, Frank (Dec'd)	Discovered many of the great jazz musicians
Torme, Mel	Singer, Composer, Pictures, Television Director-Producer
Tham, Duane	Perfomred many name Orchestras and Bands
Trace, Al	Singer, Composer
Wettling, George	Paul Whiteman, performed many famous Name Bands

The students' names have been listed in the previous pages.

Messages from Friends

Carmine Appice

Maurie and Jan always treated me great. Being I was a Ludwig endorsee I was in Chicago a lot. The greatest thing was going out to eat with them. But I want to talk about the day I was at Franks looking for a China cymbal in 1973. Maurie took me into the back room and showed me these great OLD China's from China- they sounded GREAT! I bought one for $50.00. I broke it soon after so from then on Franks Drum Shop would have to ship me China cymbals all over the States while I was touring with Beck (Jeff). This became quite a job, but they came through all the time. I miss them in Chicago and think about Franks Drum Shop every time I go to Chicago."

John H Beck

"It was 1956 at the Mid-West Band Clinic when I walked into Franks in this uniform. Maurie took me back to the sound room and we had a great time- I'll never forget it."

(Above) John H Beck, Professor of Percussion (Eastman School of Music), Timpanist, Rochester Philharmonic Orchestra

(Right) Staff Sergeant John Beck, percussionist, United States Marine Band, Washington, D.C.

James Blades, O.B.E.

"I first made the acquaintance of Maurice Lishon at The Percussive Arts Society Convention in Arizona in 1978. I was instantly impressed by his vitality and friendly approach, also by the charm of his wife Jan (his mentor). PASIC was followed by a short stay with him and also the ebullient and legendary Roy C Knapp who, as my guide, made Franks Drum Shop our first call. Here I was greeted by Maurice who introduced me to the several leading Chicago percussionists present, including George Gaber of Indiana University. My immediate assessment of 'Maurie's' emporium was that here was a 'Percussionists' Mecca'. The stock included almost every known percussion instrument, for sale or hire, and his collection of percussion literature was, I felt certain, then unparalleled. In addition to his stock and his fair dealing as a supplier Maurice, with his years of experience as a player, was able and willing to advise where he felt neccessary.

As a host he knew all the best places for coffee and those where the pancakes were most heavily loaded. He also (as did Roy Knapp) seemed to know almost every citizen of Chicago and they Roy and himself."

(Above) James Blades in 1963
(from the film "We Make Music")

(Right) James Blades with his wife Jean, arriving at Nonsuch Manor for his 90th birthday celebration on 9-9-91.
   The Rolls-Royce was loaned by Alan Taylor, timpanist of the Royal Opera House, Covent Garden, London.

Hal Blaine

"The year was 1948. I was a new recruit at the Roy Knapp school of percussion. Studying with Roy and all the great teachers of the era. To say that I was excited would be an understatement. After meeting most of the 500 or so students I set out looking for a drum shop to hang. Living at the old Majestic Hotel in the Loop there was only one shop to consider.. Franks... I walked in off of the street, a total unknown, and was treated like a Gene Krupa or a Louis Bellson. Maurie was like a father to us all. His words of wisdom have stayed with me for all these years... "Hard work and study will put you at the top!" He was right and for me the rest is history. His cordial manner and sense of humor helped me more than I can say. (Being Jewish didn't help either; he treated the goyem the same way... like gentlemen.)

I recently saw Maurie and his lovely lady at a NAMM show and was really delighted to see him looking so good. Let's all say a prayer for Maurie, "Lord please give him another 39 years!" "

Ed Thigpen

"In the early days of my career, that is the 1950's, I didn't get to Chicago very often. I think I first met the Lishon's in the 60's when I was with Oscar Peterson. Although I was not a Chicago resident, I do remember visiting Franks Drum Shop several times and was always greeted very warmly.

The first time I really had a chance to talk at length with Maurie and Jan wasn't until 1968 I think. I was in Chicago at the Palmer House with Ella Fitzgerald; it was then that the spirits clicked. I can remember very clearly the genuine, sincere care that both Maurie and Jan projected when they spoke. It was one of those feelings that one receives and wishes to carry and pass on to others.

I think it is important for all of us, at any age or position to be treated kindly and made to feel like we are at least a little special from time to time. It's healthy nourishment for the ego and soul. Maurie and Jan were then, and still continue to be, the personification of caring souls in their everyday association with people. May our good Lord keep them in his care."

Sincerely
Ed Thigpen

Roy Burns

"Maurie- Thanks for your advice and help on my career. You were like a second father to me. The clinics I did for you remain among my favorites."

All the best,
Roy Burns

(Below) Roy and Maurie, FDS clinic c. 1968

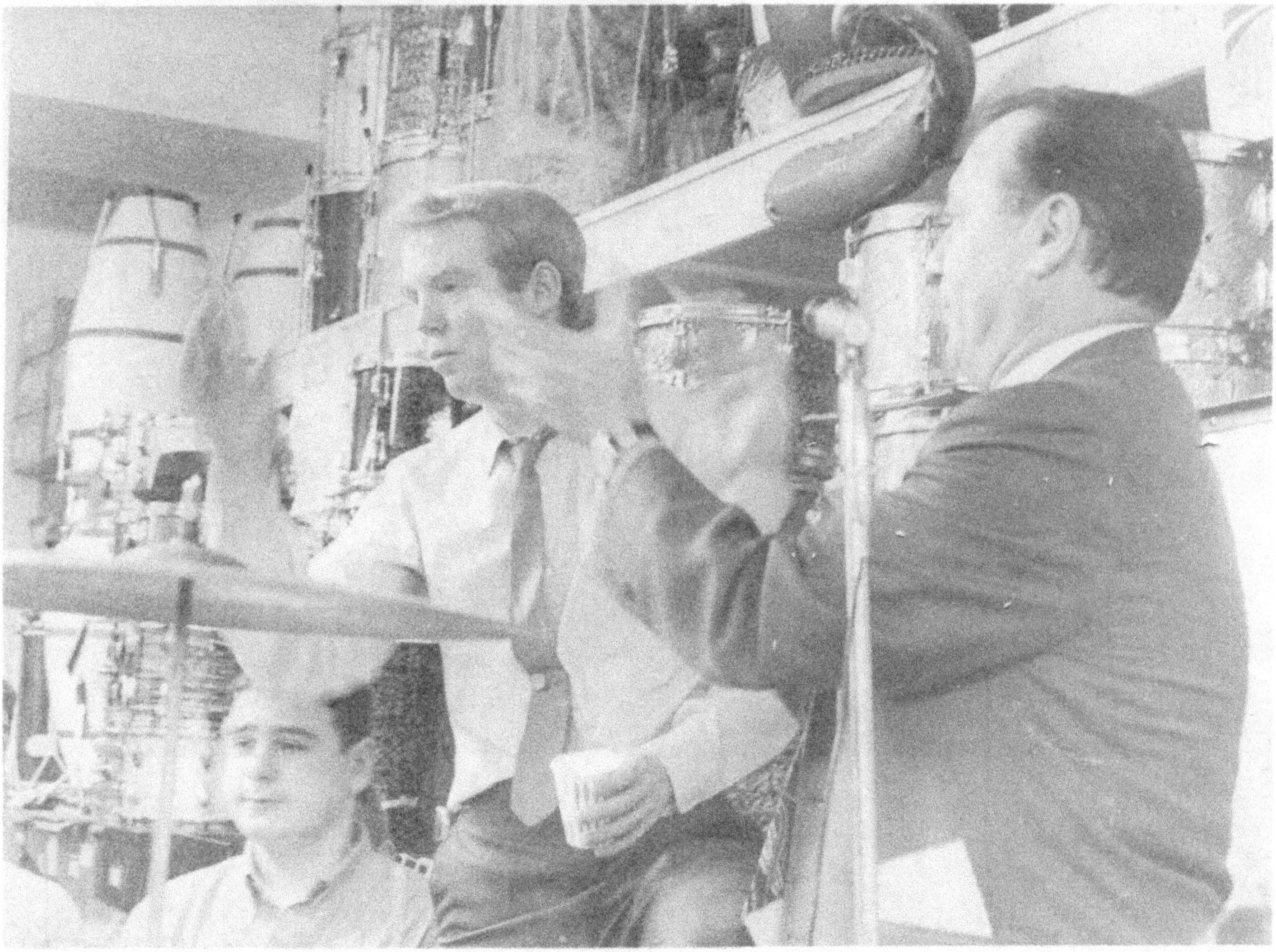

Joe Calato

"The year was 1960 and Regal Tip drumsticks had been on the market approximately 2-3 years. The nylon tip that I had invented was winning favor with drummers throughout the world.

It was a dreary day and my mood was like the weather when my wife presented me with a letter from Franks Drum Shop. What I thought was going to be a nice purchase order turned out to be a tongue lashing, with a few expletives thrown in, from Maurie Lishon wanting to know where his last order was. It was then and there that I decided to go to my first NAMM convention and make it a must to meet this crude, tough and foul-mouthed person.

Upon arriving in Chicago, a visit to Franks DrumShop was my first priority. I stepped out of the elevator and into the shop and there he was; busy talking with drummers, scooting around the store, and taking care of two or three customers at a time. There he was, all 5'2" of him, puffing on a big fat black cigar when I overheard him say to a customer rolling some sticks on the counter, "Hey, the sticks are straight, the glass is crooked!" This quote was one of thousands that I have heard from him since.

Within five minutes of introducing myself I began to realize that this man was one of the kindest, warmest, and most sincere persons I have ever or will ever have known. Then he introduced me to his wife Jan. Well, this charming, beautiful and warm lady was the other 50% of what made Franks Drum Shop one of the most popular drummers quarters throughout the world.

To this day there had been a friendship and love within our two families that will live with all of us until we depart from the earth. Thank God for Maurie and Jan."

Bun E Carlos

"Franks restored vintage (painted) snare drums for me. They sold me my first custom drum set; a Slingerland set with copper hardware. The shop once loaned me a white pearl Radio King kit for eighteen months! Chuck shot five videos for Cheap Trick at the "Night Gallery" in Waukegan for our first album. We did 'em all in one afternoon- quite a change from nowadays!! I'll always have great memories of Franks!"

Barrett Deems

"I gave the first drum clinic in the '50's at the old shop at 218 S. Wabash. I remember that Don Osborne, then president of Slingerland, was there. I have known the Lishon family for over 40 years."

BARRETT DEEMS ORCHESTRA
SALUTE TO GENE KRUPA

Barrett & Friends .... Gene Krupa, Buddy Rich
The World's Greatest Drum Soloists

The Barrett Deems Big Band, 1991

Peter Erskine

(Above) c. 1968
(Above right) c. 1974
(Below right) 1993

"Even though I come originally from New Jersey, I went to high school in Michigan and college at Indiana University, so I always felt like an 'honorary' Mid-Westerner. While a student at the Interlochen Arts Academy (1968-1971), there was only one place where we percussionists would consider ordering our sticks and mallets (and drum books, triangles, etc.) from: Franks Drum Shop. After knowing Franks by only it's advertisements and mail-order packages, it was a thrill to finally visit the shop, the percussion Mecca. The percussion section from the Interlochen Symphony Orchestra, attired in it's dress tour outfits, all made the pilgrimage as soon as we got to Chicago for the first time. (This was the big city!) Maurie made us all feel at home, and he made us all feel kind of important and professional, too (remember, we were high school students).

It was thrilling to see Roy Knapp's set-up and all of the other fantastic percussion instruments in Maurie's collection ("museum"). My most exciting moment came when Maurie showed me and actually let me play a set of boo-bams!"

"From that time on, I would always stop by Franks whenever I passed through Chicago. Whether for a pair of drumsticks, a cymbal, or a 'hello', Franks Drum Shop was always a drummer's home away from home. And Maurie and Jan would always come out to support (and enjoy, I hope) Chicago-area gigs... I remember their gracious presence at Stan Kenton, Maynard Ferguson, and Weather Report concerts. Their support of the drumming community was heartfelt and unparalleled."

Steve Ettleson

"Maurie was my musical father when I was growing up in Chicago. I spent as much time as I could at that shop. Maurie's advice to me was "Always play with conviction- If you're going to make a mistake, make it a big one!" I've made some big mistakes but I never regretted any of them thanks to Maurie."

Vic Firth

"To Maurie and Jan-
     Remember that first PASIC Show - Eastman School 1976?! We had a booth that was 4X4 and you sold more product than the next ten booths around us. What a talker - what a friend."

George Gaber

"Jan and Maurie Lishon are legends of their time. The love, dedication, and committment they made for drums and drumming is reknown. Teachers, students, manufacturers and musicians in many fields all felt the deft touch and warm assistance by the Lishons. Franks Drum Shop was a mecca for the local and traveling musicians from all over the globe.

The inventories were stupendous and their services outstanding. The adventures in exchanges with them were great. The Lishons provided a large drum head from Australia, a Lali log from Fiji, a wing gong sent to Banff, timpani to Aspen and cacacaxa to Indiana University. It was all part of their gigantic enterprise. I salute them and hold them in high esteem."

Don & Mary Green

"We will always remember the day that Mary and I brought our first instrument to Franks Drum Shop. Maurie was the first dealer for ROSS Mallet Instruments. His encouragement and help was instrumental in getting our mallet instrument business off the ground. We shall be ever grateful to Maurie and Jan."
  DON GREEN

"Maurie snatched Jan from a chorus line, put her upstairs on Wabash Ave in Chicago and together they became a living legend in the music business. Don and I have loved being with them and listening to the wonderful stories they have to share about their contacts with so many musicians who have become legends themselves. It's been wonderful to know them as business associates and as personal friends. The laughs can't be counted."
  MARY GREEN

Don Green (left) with Hal Trommer (now deceased), an old and good friend of the Lishon's who was with the J.C. Deagan Co. for over 30 years.

Saul Goodman

"There is a great deal of good to be said about Maurie. First of all, whenever the N.Y. Philharmonic played in Chicago I always visited Maurie and the first thing he asked me was "Can I take you out to dinner tonight?" This always happened for the number of years I've known him. In addition I have always known him to be a fine and courteous gentleman."

Jake Jerger

"Maurie and Jan- Remember 'Percuss-O-Rama' '62 at Maine West H.S. which you sponsored? It was set for 3 P.M., and at 2:45 there was hardly anyone there. Jan and Betty were out in the lobby getting nervous, and at 2:50 P.M. the people came streaming in. It was a huge success! Your support through the years to me and my students was always there. Thanks!"

(Left) Jake Jerger, 1992

(Below) Jake with Maurie at his first big percussion concert, sponsored by Franks Drum Shop.

Walt Johnston

"Maurie Lishon... he was one of the three most influential drum shop owners in the United States. He ruled the Midwest and, like the late Bob Yeager (Professional Drum Shop, Hollywood, CA) and the late Frank Ippolito (Professional Percussion Center, New York, New York), whatever lines he blessed, would gain immediate acceptance from the drum departments of general music stores across the country.

Keep in mind that back then "in the good old days" there weren't as many drum companies around. Premier was about the only visible "foreign" made drum set and 3 manufacturers in the U.S. dominated the market. The "MADE IN JAPAN" sticker was noted only for low price outfits of questionable quality."

"When the Pearl Musical Instrument Company agreed to update their products and also go after the professional market, they first got the stamp of approval from the leading Hollywood studio players. Then, the "Big 3" were approached. Franks Drum Shop was the "proof statement" for the Midwest, and once the product was in his shop with HIS stamp of approval, Pearl dealerships began opening throughout Illinois and in all the surrounding states. The amount of influence Maurie, Bob, and Frank had with the drumming community was mind-boggling. Their reccomendations were always taken seriously and a negative vote could add additional years and expense to a product introduction.

So, Maurie... even though your hands don't match and your glasses sometimes slip sideways in the sign of incredulity... "Franks" for the memories and for your help introducing Pearl! May the third time around find you still swingin'."

Walt Johnston at L.D. Heater, early '70's

Walt, unidentified geisha girl, Remo Belli

In the early 70's Pearl got started operating out of the L.D. Heater Music Company in Portland, Oregon. When Lyle Heater had a stroke, Walt was elected to to go Japan to keep the ball rolling with the Pearl Drums and the proprietary Lyle Drums made by Pearl. Remo Belli was on the same trip for other reasons, and the pair spent an interesting evening at a spa hosted by the Yanagasawa's.

Joel Leach

"Maurie's unoffical motto was, "You want WHAT? WHEN? -- OK, It'll be there!" And you know what? He never failed.

Jan's mission on earth seemed to be to stock every piece of music written for percussion as soon as she learned about it. Virtually all percussion teachers made regular treks to the shop to stock up for the coming school year.

Jan and Maurie and Franks Drum Shop led the percussion education movement not only because they had virtually everything on hand, but because they were ALWAYS willing to give of their time to help out those of us who were early entries in the university programs ourselves."

Joel Leach

These 1966 photos were taken when Joel and Owen Reed were doing research at the shop for their forthcoming CPP-Belwin book SCORING FOR PERCUSSION

From left, standing; Maurie, Owen Reed, Clarence Williams, Chuck Lishon, and Joel Leach. Seated: Jan Lishon and Roy Knapp.

Larry Linkin

"Dear Maurie,
    I've still got your half of the $10.00.
        -Link"

Aldo Mazza

"I just met Maurie and Jan Lishon as a tudent at the Ludwig Percussion Syposium in the summer of 1973. At the time, I was a non-reading rock drummer with no mallet or percussion schooling whatsoever. It was to be a turning point in my life. After being exposed to intensive sessions with Gary Burton, Joe Morello, Carmine Appice and others, I went to Maurie's shop. I told Maurie I would like to take a Musser vibe back home with me but had no money. I had just met him, but he told me to take the instrument and pay him when I could. Within a week we had become very close and he treated me like a son. I was so floored by his willingness to help me that though he may not realize it, it influenced me FOR LIFE! Thank you Maurie and Jan. You helped me tremendously when it counted and you have always inspired me just by BEING these and being the way you both are. I consider myself blessed for having crossed your paths. We have kept in touch over the years and I can say that to this day part of our successes are due in some part to the sincerety and love you shared with those fortunate enough to have met you."

Lloyd McCausland

"I've had the pleasure of knowing the Lishon's for some 25 or 30 years prior to entering the business world with Remo. My associations with the Lishon's through the 24 years I've been employed by Remo, Inc. have made very clear to me that Maurie Lishon, through his Franks Drum Shop of Chicago has contributed immensely to the percussion world.

It was the one "IN" place to hang out and to see some of the greatest performers and heavyweight personalities in the industry."

Dr Ben F Miller

BEN MILLER, 1960

"I have known Maurie and Jan since 1960. I call them (and consider them) my "musical Mom and Dad". I grew up in the suburbs of Chicago and started hanging out at Franks when I was in the 6th grade. It just so happens that David Samuels and I grew up around the corner from each other and we used to go down to the shop often. We would be there for hours looking in drawers and behind counters, banging on cymbals, showing our hot licks on practice pads, slapping congas, etc.

While in college, I would usually take my girlfriends to meet Maurie and Jan before I would take them to meet my parents."

Gordon Peters

"When I think of Maurie and Jan in connection with FDS, I thing of Frienship, Dedication, Service, and Love. When I was the first official president of PAS in the early 60's, I cannot tell you what a wonderful aid these two folks were for me in trying to establish a sound percussion organization and to "weave" my way through all the personalities involved! The first thing that comes to mind is about their service response. At the Chicago Symphony Orchestra, often "The Maestro of the Moment" would decide he wanted something special with percussion; I would call Maurie at 9:15 A.M. with my request, and it would be delivered by 10:00 A.M. the same day! To have knowledge and experience embodied in a "drum dealer" was one of our Chicago treasures. A word about Jan: she was the "librarian". She kept a very complete and up-to-date stock of music and method books unparalleled at the time. This was indeed "The Complete Drum Shop"."

(Above) 1960's

(Right) 1992

Ted Reed

"Jan and Maurie Lishon had been buying my drum books for many years. We finally met at the opening of the new Avedis Zildjian Cymbal Co. factory in Norwell, MA in 1972.

We have been good friends for all these years. Maurie has a birthday coming up on August 7th - I have his birthday card ready to go. Happy Birthday, Maurie!"

Ted Reed

(Above) Ted Reed, 1993

(Right) Ted Reed, NYC, 1959

Emil Richards

"I've known Maurie and Jan for over 25 years. I consider Maurie as a father to me, and I must say I've learned the music 'business' from him. His son Marty is like a brother to me, and a percussion gathering anywhere is only complete when Maurie and Jan are on the scene."

Denny Seiwell

"I first met Maurie at Franks Drum Shop in 1963 while I was in the Navy Band stationed at the Great Lakes. It was through that meeting that I began to study drums with Roy Knapp. Years later after leaving McCartney and Wings I was to live in Chicago again for one year in 1976, while producing a local act for RCA and doing concert tours with that act. It was then that I had a chance to renew my friendship with the Lishons. I remember once needing a powerful, loud snare drum for touring, and Marty was working in the shop at the time- he gave me a beautiful Ludwig black beauty to try! That's the kind of relationship the store had with most of the pros and regulars. I'm very grateful to have been a small part of a wonderful place like Franks Drum Shop, and to have known the Lishons. Thanks forever!"

Gideon Steiner

"I was 21 years old, just married, just joining the Israel Philharmonic Orchestra, my first concert tour abroad..... Oh God.... 33 years ago. My monthly salary then was $125.00. Yes, one hundred and twenty-five American dollars per month. How shall we survive with that money? In Chicago, looking for a xylophone I went in to Franks Drum Shop. Me: "How much is this used Deagan?" Maurie: "Five hundred U.S. dollars." Me: "I don't have that money." Maurie: "How much do you have?" Me: "One hundred U.S. dollars." Maurie: "You want it? Yes! It is yours...."

This was Maurie. Dear Jan who never stopped reccommending to me beautiful percussion music.

That old Deagan xylophone really helped me for many, many years. By the way, Maurie, thank you for shipping those Ludwig timps to Rio de Janeiro.... I always loved the two of you like second parents."

Robert Zildjian

"Frank's Drum shop started in 1938. Under Frank Gault, it became a mecca for all traveling drummers as well as the great Chicago bunch- Roy Knapp, Maurie, Dave Tough, Bobby Christian- the list goes on and on. I learned so much from Frank and his repairman Stuart. Frank finally decided to retire and failed in two successors- Joe Berryman wanted to teach and play; Milt Chalifoix really wanted to quit retail completely.

Finally in came the only couple who could really succeed such a great personality- Maurie and Jan. We all complained when they organized the inventory, we all complained when they took Frank's old trombone out of the toilet, when they organized the music department (Jan's hard work) - most of us had a certain degree of skepticism and all of us were delighted when the years came and went and Franks Drum Shop grew and grew. When Jan and Maurie decided to quit it really was the end of an era for me and all that 226 South Wabash meant to me. Chicago has never been the same.

But everything changes... Look at SABIAN, the youngest cymbal company in the world!"

(Left) Robert Zildjian at age 30 in the 1950's.
  photo by Vito Pascucci
(Below) Robert (age 68) and Willi Zildjian at
  the 10th Sabian Anniversary, Frankfurt, 1992.
  photo by Lissa Wales

The Lishon family (from left): Michael, Suzanne, Jan, Marty, Maurie, "B.J."

My sister thanks you
My brother thanks you
My father thanks you
My mother thanks you
And I thank you......
For the pleasure
of your company.....

Chuck Lishon 1941 - 1978

Aleta Lishon   Chuck Lishon

REBEATS PUBLICATIONS
visit the Rebeats website or contact us for details

THE GRETSCH DRUM BOOK
by Rob Cook
with John Sheridan
Business history, dating guide

THE SLINGERLAND BOOK
by Rob Cook
Business history, dating guide

THE ROGERS BOOK
by Rob Cook
Business history, dating guide

THE LUDWIG BOOK
by Rob Cook
Business history, dating guide

THE MAKING OF A DRUM COMPANY
The autobiography of Wm. F. Ludwig II, with Rob Cook

BEST SEAT IN THE HOUSE
Memoir of Humble Pie's Jerry Shirley

THE LEEDY WAY
Biography of George Way, History of Leedy, Camco, Conn, L&S

MY LIFE IN PERCUSSION
Five Decades In The Music Products Industry
Karl Dustman memoir

HAL BLAINE & THE WRECKING CREW
Memoir of Hal Blaine, with Mr. Bonzai

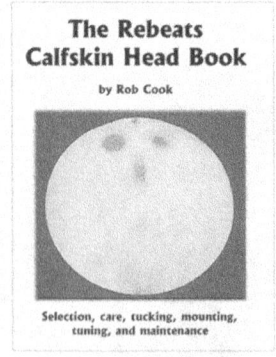
THE REBEATS CALFSKIN HEAD BOOK

George Way mini-biography, vendor directory

GENE KRUPA, HIS LIFE AND TIMES
biography of Gene Krupa, by Bruce Crowther

THE BABY DODDS STORY
Memoir of Baby Dodds, as told to Larry Gara

Gretsch 1941 Catalog Reprint

P.O. Box 6, Alma, Michigan 48801
989 463 4757
www.Rebeats.com   rob@rebeats.com

www.ingramcontent.com/pod-product-compliance
Lightning Source LLC
Chambersburg PA
CBHW081348080526
44588CB00016B/2415